BLESSED ARE the PURE of HEART

Catechesis on the Sermon on the Mount and Writings of St. Paul

BLESSED ARE the PURE of HEART

Catechesis on the Sermon on the Mount and Writings of St. Paul

JOHN PAUL II

Preface by Donald W. Wuerl

ST. PAUL EDITIONS

Reprinted with permission of *L'Osservatore Romano,*
English edition.

Library of Congress Cataloging in Publication Data

John Paul II, Pope, 1920-
    Blessed are the pure of heart.

    Includes index.
    1. Catholic Church—Sermons. 2. Sermons, English.
I. Title.
BX1756.J64B57   1983   241'.66   83-7221

ISBN 0-8198-1110-6 cloth
      0-8198-1111-4 paper

Printed in the U.S.A. by the Daughters of St. Paul
50 St. Paul's Ave., Boston, MA 02130

The Daughters of St. Paul are an international congregation
of religious women serving the Church with the communications media.

CONTENTS

PREFACE

The Second Vatican Council speaks of the human situation with all its infirmities in the struggle to reach God, "In order to establish peace and communion between sinful human beings and Himself, as well as to fashion them into a fraternal community, God determined to intervene in human history in a way both new and definitive...that He might reconcile the world to Himself" (The Church's Missionary Activity, no. 3). Christ's reconciliation has a long way to go to reach its goal. The new man and the old man of St. Paul still live side by side, each one vying for the chance to win the day.

It is the duty of the Church to nourish and feed the fragile new life that has been conceived by Christ and born in His Church. This is done, in the context of a world only partly perfect—only on the way to its goal of perfection in Christ. "The Church, God's only flock, like a standard lifted high for the nations to see, ministers the gospel of peace as she makes her pilgrim way in hope toward her goal, the fatherland above" (Decree on Ecumenism, no. 2).

Christ gave men His love. But He did not outline each detail of the road that leads to its full possession. In fact, He spoke of it as if it

were not a love with which we are familiar. Part
of the problem for the Christian in attaining this
gift is precisely that of defining exactly what
love it is that Christ offers. This is so since His
love seems to involve some ambiguity. The
pages of the Gospels are filled with words that
Christ uses one way and we use in another.
These words also involve us in what seems like
contradictions.

The voices in the Gospels tell us that Jesus
saw peace as many-sided. In Matthew 26:52,
Christ warns against the use of force. Yet He applies it Himself as He clears out the Temple (Jn.
2:14-17). At times, His position even seems
threatening.

"Do not suppose that I have come to bring
peace to the earth: it is not peace I have come to
bring, but a sword. For I have come to set a man
against his father, a daughter against her
mother, a daughter-in-law against her mother-
in-law. A man's enemies will be his own
household" (Mt. 10:34-36).

He told His followers to be peacemakers but
reminded them that His peace is not of this
world. In the Sermon on the Mount, Jesus an-
nounced what He would ask of His followers. He
stated the new level of ethical awareness He
would demand from His kingdom. His peace
was to be a challenge.

"You have heard that it was said of the
people in the old days, 'You shall not kill....'
I say to you that anyone who is angry with his
brother must stand trial.... 'You shall love your

neighbor and hate your enemy....' But I say to you, 'Love your enemies, and pray for those who persecute you' " (Mt. 5:21-29).

By involving men in a new ethical situation contradicting their own experience, Christ set the stage for the working out of His plan. But He also watered the seeds of tension. In contrast to the pragmatic calculations and reasoned positions of the Greeks and Romans, Jesus spoke of a personal commitment in charity toward all men. So revolutionary and demanding is this commitment that it depends utterly on a perspective offered only by revelation. And so Christian love is part of, as well as the result of, revelation. But it is a revelation that must be acted on in terms of this world.

Matthew outlines, in the several chapters that make up the Sermon on the Mount, some of the essential attitudes that are the result of the new perspective. The Gospel insists on a vision of man as an eventual citizen of heaven. The balance Christ sets is between works of the social order and those directed to another world. The background is always human life seen as potentially divine and eternal. He proclaims peace in the same breath with which He blesses poverty and mourning. Believers are reminded of their duties before the poor, the afflicted, the downtrodden, but always in terms of the kingdom of heaven. The perspective is that of their vocations as sons of God. They are to build up this world because they are called to see God. Within this view, both God and man have value in themselves. The Sermon on the Mount requires that the believer see his fellow-man's dignity. This dignity comes from God, resides in man, and is held sacred because of man's ultimate goal—union with God. But such a perspective requires faith. Belief alone makes it possible for a man to hold out hope in the life to come. Faith provides the moral climate in which, for the Christian, human dignity can assert itself and human freedom can grow.

If each life is potentially eternal, if each man is potentially a son of God, then the claims of violence against Him must take a secondary place. Gabriel Marcel once spoke to this point in reference to the Christian faith in the life to come: "...the world today can be endured only if one's spirit is riveted on hope in the resurrection. For us Christians living today, something especially influences us to believe in the resurrection of the body: it is, for example, what we know the body endured in the concentration camps. One feels that human flesh has undergone such intolerable outrage that it must receive some kind of reparation in glory.... I believe life today is unendurable if one's spirit is not rooted in the hope of our creed. If this hope were shared by a greater number, perhaps a respect for the flesh and for the body, so terribly lacking in our time, would be restored."

This same perspective obtains when we speak of the Christian vision of love. Christ's love must be seen within the context of His revelation, which includes our life eternal.

The Church has always understood that the difficulty surrounding love must be seen with the paradox of the crucifixion. The world has its ways. Revelation has presented another. For the believer, the direction and style of life that the cross speaks, even with its paradoxes, must be the only way.

In this collection of talks on the mystery of Christ's love and human love, Pope John Paul presents for us a clear and consistent teaching. His synthesis of perennial human problems, the constant teaching of the Magisterium and his own personal reflections on the experiences of our day is a welcome guide to all who look to the Holy Father for insight and counsel.

This volume reminds us of the duty and function of the Holy See to teach and lead God's people. It also points out very clearly how well Pope John Paul understands and accomplishes this divinely appointed mission.

—*Rev. Msgr. Donald W. Wuerl*

Christ Appeals
to Man's Heart

General audience of April 16, 1980.

1. As the subject of our future reflections—at the Wednesday meetings—I wish to develop the following statement of Christ, which is part of the Sermon on the Mount: "You have heard that it was said, You shall not commit adultery. But I say to you that everyone who looks at a woman lustfully has already committed adultery with her in his heart" (Mt. 5:27-28).

This passage seems to have a key meaning for the theology of the body, like the one in which Christ referred to the "beginning," and which served as the basis of the preceding analyses. We were then able to realize how wide was the context of a sentence, or rather of a word, uttered by Christ. It was a question not only of the immediate context, which emerged in the course of the conversation with the Pharisees, but of the global context, which we cannot penetrate without going back to the first chapters of the Book of Genesis (omitting what refers there to the other books of the Old Testament). The preceding analyses have shown how extensive is the content that Christ's reference to the "beginning" involves.

NEED OF FULFILLMENT
OF THE LAW

The statement, to which we are now referring, that is, Matthew 5:27-28, will certainly
introduce us—not only to the immediate context in which it appears—but also to its wider
context, the global context, through which the
key-meaning of the theology of the body will be
revealed to us. This statement is one of the
passages of the Sermon on the Mount in which
Jesus Christ makes a fundamental revision of
the way of understanding and carrying out the
moral law of the Old Covenant. It refers, in
order, to the following commandments of the
Decalogue: the fifth, "you shall not kill" (cf.
Mt. 5:21-26), the sixth, "You shall not commit
adultery" (cf. Mt. 5:27-32)—it is significant that
at the end of this passage there also appears the
question of the "certificate of divorce" (cf. Mt.
5:31-32), already mentioned in the preceding
chapter—and the eighth commandment according to the text of Exodus (cf. Ex. 20:7): "You
shall not swear falsely, but shall perform to the
Lord what you have sworn" (cf. Mt. 5:33-37).

Significant, above all, are the words that
precede these articles—and the following ones
—of the Sermon on the Mount, the words in
which Jesus declares: "Think not that I have
come to abolish the law and the prophets, I have
come not to abolish them but to fulfill them"
(Mt. 5:17). In the sentences that follow, Jesus
explains the meaning of this opposition and the

necessity of the "fulfillment" of the law in order to realize the kingdom of God: "Whoever... does them (these commandments) and teaches them shall be called great in the kingdom of heaven" (Mt. 5:19). "The kingdom of heaven" means the kingdom of God in the eschatological dimension.

The fulfillment of the law conditions, fundamentally, this kingdom in the temporal dimension of human existence. It is a question, however, of a fulfillment that fully corresponds to the meaning of the law, of the Decalogue, of the individual commandments. Only this fulfillment constructs that justice which God the Legislator willed. Christ the Teacher urges us not to give such a human interpretation of the whole law and the individual commandments contained in it that it does not construct the justice willed by God the Legislator: "Unless your righteousness exceeds that of the scribes and Pharisees, you will never enter the kingdom of heaven" (Mt. 5:20).

ASPECTS OF FULFILLMENT

2. In this context there appears Christ's statement according to Matthew 5:27-28, which we intend to take as the basis for the present analyses, considering it, together with the other statement according to Matthew 19:3-9 (and Mk. 10), as the key to the theology of the body. Like the other one, this one has an explicitly normative character. It confirms the principle

of human morality contained in the commandment, "You shall not commit adultery," and, at the same time, it determines an appropriate and full understanding of this principle, that is, an understanding of the foundation and at the same time of the condition for its adequate "fulfillment." The latter is to be considered precisely in the light of the words of Matthew 5:17-20, already quoted before, to which we have just drawn attention.

It is a question here, on the one hand, of adhering to the meaning that God the Legislator enclosed in the commandment, "You shall not commit adultery," and, on the other hand, of carrying out that "justice" on the part of man, a justice that must "superabound" in man himself, that is, it must reach its specific fullness in him. These are, so to speak, the two aspects of "fulfillment" in the evangelical sense.

AT THE HEART OF "ETHOS"

3. We find ourselves in this way at the heart of *ethos,* that is, in what can be defined as the interior form, almost the soul, of human morality. Contemporary thinkers (e.g., Scheler) see in the Sermon on the Mount a great turning-point in the field of *ethos.*[1] A living morality, in the existential sense, is not formed only by the norms that invest the form of the commandments, precepts and prohibitions, as in the case of "You shall not commit adultery." The morality in which there is realized the very meaning

of being a man—which is, at the same time, the fulfillment of the law by means of the "super-abounding" of justice through subjective vital-ity—is formed in the interior perception of values, from which there springs duty as the expression of conscience, as the response of one's own personal "ego." At the same time *ethos* makes us enter the depth of the norm itself and descend within the man-subject of morality. Moral value is connected with the dynamic process of man's intimacy. To reach it, it is not enough to stop "at the surface" of human actions, it is necessary to pene-trate inside.

INTERIOR JUSTICE

4. In addition to the commandment, "You shall not commit adultery," the Decalogue has also, "You shall not covet your neighbor's wife."[2] In the Sermon on the Mount, Christ con-nects them with each other, in a way: "Every-one who looks at a woman lustfully has already committed adultery with her in his heart." However, it is not a question so much of dis-tinguishing the scope of those two command-ments of the Decalogue as of pointing out the dimension of the interior action, referred to also in the words: "You shall not commit adultery."

This action finds its visible expression in the "act of the body," an act in which the man and the woman participate against the law of matrimonial exclusiveness. The casuistry of the books of the Old Testament, which aimed at

investigating what, according to exterior criteria, constituted this "act of the body" and
was, at the same time, directed at combatting
adultery, opened to the latter various legal
"loopholes."[3] In this way, on the basis of the
multiple compromises "for hardness of heart"
(Mt. 19:8), the meaning of the commandment,
willed by the Legislator, underwent a distortion. People kept to legalistic observance of the
formula, which did not "superabound" in the
interior justice of hearts.

Christ shifts the essence of the problem to
another dimension, when He says: "Everyone
who looks at a woman lustfully has already
committed adultery with her in his heart"
(according to ancient translations: "has already
made her an adulteress in his heart," a formula
which seems to be more exact).[4]

In this way, therefore, Christ appeals to the
interior man. He does so several times and
under different circumstances. In this case it
seems particularly explicit and eloquent, not
only with regard to the configuration of
evangelical *ethos*, but also with regard to the
way of viewing man. It is not only the ethical
reason, therefore, but also the anthropological
one, that makes it advisable to dwell at greater
length on the text of Matthew 5:27-28, which
contains the words spoken by Christ in the Sermon on the Mount.

FOOTNOTES

1. Ich kenne kein grandioseres Zeugnis für eine solche Neuerschliessung eines ganzen Werbereiches, die das ältere Ethos relativiert, als die Bergpredigt, die auch in ihrer Form als Zeugnis solcher Neuerschliessung und Relativierung der älteren "Gesetzes"-werte sich überall kundgibt: "Ich aber sage euch" (Max Scheler, *Der Formalismus in der Ethik und die materiale Wertethik*, Halle a.d.S., Verlag M. Niemeyer, 1921, p. 316, no. 1).

2. Cf. Ex. 20:17; Dt. 5:21.

3. On this point, see the continuation of the present meditations.

4. The text of the Vulgate offers a faithful translation of the original: *iam moechatus est eam in corde suo*. In fact, the Greek verb *moicheúo* is transitive. In modern European languages, on the other hand, "to commit adultery" is an intransitive verb; so we get the translation: "has committed adultery *with* her." And thus,

—*in Italian*: "...ha già commesso adulterio con lei nel suo cuore" (Version of the Italian Episcopal Conference, 1971; similarly the version of the Pontifical Biblical Institute, 1961, and the one prepared by S. Garofalo, 1966).

—*in French*: "...a déjà commis, dans son coeur, l'adultère avec elle" (Bible de Jérusalem, Paris, 1973; Traduction Oecuménique, Paris, 1972; Crampon); only Fillion translates: "A déjà commis l'adultere dans son coeur."

—*in English*: "has already committed adultery with her in his heart" (Douay Version, 1582, similarly Revised Standard Version, from 1611 to 1966; R. Knox, New English Bible, Jerusalem Bible, 1966).

—*in German*: "...hat in seinem Herzen schon Ehebruch mit ihr begangen" (Einheitsübersetzung der Heiligen Schrift, im Auftrag der Bischöfe des deutschen Sprachbereiches, 1979).

—*in Spanish*: "...ya cometió adulterio con ella en su corazón" (Bibl. Societ., 1966).

—*in Portuguese*: "...já cometeu adulterio com ela no seu coraçaõ" (M. Soares, Sao Paolo, 1933).

—*in Polish*: ancient translations: "...już ją scudzołożył w sercu swoim"; last translation: "...już się w swoim ser cu dopuścił z nią cudzołóstwa" (Biblia Tysiąclecia).

Ethical and Anthropological Content of the Commandment: "Do Not Commit Adultery!"

General audience of April 23, 1980.

1. Let us recall the words of the Sermon on the Mount, to which we are referring in this cycle of our Wednesday reflections: "You have heard"—the Lord says—"that it was said: You shall not commit adultery. But I say to you that everyone who looks at a woman lustfully has already committed adultery with her in his heart" (Mt. 5:27-28).

The man to whom Jesus refers here is precisely "historical" man, the one whose "beginning" and "theological prehistory" we traced in the preceding series of analyses. Directly, it is the one who hears with his own ears the Sermon on the Mount. But together with him, there is also every other man, set before that moment of history, both in the immense space of the past, and in the equally vast one of the future. To this "future," confronted with the Sermon on the Mount, there belongs also our present, our contemporary age.

This man is, in a way, "every" man, "each" of us. Both the man of the past and also the man of the future can be the one who knows the positive commandment "you shall not commit adultery" as "contained in the Law" (cf. Rom. 2:22-23), but he can equally be the one who, according to the Letter to the Romans, has this commandment only "written on his heart" (cf. Rom. 2:15).[1] In the light of the previous reflections, he is the man who from his "beginning" has acquired a precise sense of the meaning of the body, already before crossing "the threshold" of his historical experiences, in the very mystery of creation, since he emerged from it as "male and female" (Gn. 1:27). He is the historical man, who, at the "beginning" of his earthly vicissitudes, found himself "inside" the knowledge of good and evil, breaking the covenant with his Creator. He is the male-man, who "knew" (the woman) his wife and "knew" her several times, and "she conceived and bore" (cf. Gn. 4:1-2) according to the Creator's plan, which went back to the state of original innocence (cf. Gn. 1:28; 2:24).

ENTERING INTO HIS FULL IMAGE

2. In His Sermon on the Mount, particularly in the words of Matthew 5:27-28, Christ addresses precisely that man. He addresses the man of a given moment of history and, at the same time, all men, belonging to the same human history. He addresses, as we have already seen, the "interior" man. Christ's words have an explicit anthropological con-

tent; they concern those perennial meanings, through which an "adequate" anthropology is constituted.

These words, by means of their ethical content, simultaneously constitute such an anthropology, and demand, so to speak, that man should enter into his full image. The man who is "flesh," and who as a male remains in relationship, through his body and sex, with woman (also the expression "you shall not commit adultery" indicates this, in fact), must, in the light of these words of Christ, find himself again interiorly, in his "heart." [2] The "heart" is this dimension of humanity with which the sense of the meaning of the human body, and the order of this sense, is directly linked. It is a question, here, both of the meaning which, in preceding analyses, we called "nuptial," and of that which we denominated "generative." And of what order are we treating?

MEANING OF ADULTERY

3. This part of our considerations must give an answer precisely to this question—an answer that reaches not only the ethical reasons, but also the anthropological; they remain, in fact, in a mutual relationship. For the time being, preliminarily, it is necessary to establish the meaning of the text of Matthew 5:7-28, the meaning of the expressions used in it and their mutual relationship.

Adultery, to which the aforesaid commandment refers, means a breach of the unity, by means of which man and woman only as husband and wife, can unite so closely as to be "one flesh" (Gn. 2:24). Man commits adultery if he unites in this way with a woman who is not his wife. The woman likewise commits adultery if she unites in this way with a man who is not her husband. It must be deduced from this that the "adultery in the heart," committed by the man when he "looks at a woman lustfully," means a quite definite interior act. It is a question of a desire directed, in this case, by the man towards a woman who is not his wife, in order to unite with her as if she were, that is—using once more the words of Genesis 2:4—in such a way that "they become one flesh." This desire, as an interior act, is expressed by means of the sense of sight, that is, with looks, as in the case of David and Bathsheba, to use an example taken from the Bible (cf. 2 Sm. 11:2).[3] The connection of lust with the sense of sight has been highlighted particularly in Christ's words.

MAN'S INTERIOR ACT

4. These words do not say clearly whether the woman—the object of lust—is the wife of another or whether simply she is not the wife of the man who looks at her in this way. She may be the wife of another, or even not bound by marriage. It is necessary rather to intuit it, on the basis particularly of the expression which, precisely, defines as adultery what man has committed "in his heart" with his look. It must be correctly deduced that this lustful look, if

addressed to his own wife, is not adultery "in his heart," precisely because the man's interior act refers to the woman who is his wife, with regard to whom adultery cannot take place. If the conjugal act as an exterior act, in which "they become one flesh," is lawful in the relationship of the man in question with the woman who is his wife, in like manner also the interior act in the same relationship is in conformity with morality.

CLARIFYING THE TEXT

5. Nevertheless, that desire, indicated by the expression "everyone who looks at a woman lustfully," has a biblical and theological dimension of its own, which we cannot but clarify here. Even if this dimension is not manifested directly in this one concrete expression of Matthew 5:27-28, it is, however, deeply rooted in the global context, which refers to the revelation of the body. We must go back to this context, in order that Christ's appeal "to the heart," to the interior man, may ring out in all the fullness of its truth.

The statement of the Sermon on the Mount quoted (Mt. 5:27-28) has fundamentally an indicative character. The fact that Christ directly addresses man as the one "who looks at a woman lustfully," does not mean that His words, in their ethical meaning, do not refer also to woman. Christ expresses Himself in this way to illustrate with a concrete example how "the fulfillment of the law" must be understood, according to the meaning that God the Legislator gave to it, and furthermore how that "superabounding of justice" in the man who observes the sixth commandment of the Decalogue, must be understood.

Speaking in this way, Christ wants us not to dwell on the example in itself, but to penetrate the full ethical and anthropological meaning of the statement. If it has an indicative character, this means that, following its traces, we can arrive at understanding the general truth about "historical" man, which is valid also for the theology of the body. The further stages of our reflections will have the purpose of bringing us closer to understanding this truth.

FOOTNOTES

1. In this way, the content of our reflections shifts, in a way, to the field of "natural law." The words quoted from the Letter to the Romans (2:15) have always been considered, in revelation, as a source of confirmation for the existence of natural law. Thus the concept of natural law also acquires a theological meaning.

Cf. among others, D. Composta, *Teologia del diritto naturale*, status quaestionis, Brescia 1972 (Ed. Civilta), pp. 7-22, 41-53; J. Fuchs, S.J., *Lex naturae. Zur Theologie des Naturrechts*, Düsseldorf 1955, pp. 22-30; E. Hamel, S.J., *Loi naturelle et loi du Christ*, Bruges-Paris 1964 (Desclee de Brouwer) p. 18; A. Sacchi, "La legge naturale nella Bibbia" in: *La legge naturale. Le relazioni del Convegno dei teologi moralisti dell'Italia settentrionale* (September 11-13, 1969), Bologna, 1970 (Ed. Dehoniane), p. 53; F. Böckle, "La legge naturale e la legge cristiana," *ibid.*, pp. 214-215; A. Feuillet, "Le fondement de la morale ancienne et chrétienne d'apres l'Epitre aux Romains," *Revue*

Thomiste 78 (1970) 357-386; Th. Herr, *Naturrecht aus der kritischen Sicht des Neuen Testaments*, München 1976 (Schöning) pp. 155-164.

2. "The typically Hebraic usage reflected in the New Testament implies an understanding of man as unity of thought, will and feeling. (...) It depicts man as a whole, viewed from his intentionality; *the heart as the center of man is thought of as source of will, emotion, thoughts and affections.*

This traditional Judaic conception was related by Paul to Hellenistic categories, such as "mind," "attitude," "thoughts" and "desires." Such a coordination between the Judaic and Hellenistic categories is found in Phil. 1:7, 4:7; Rom. 1:21-24, where "heart" is thought of as the center from which these things flow (R. Jewett, *Paul's Anthropological Terms. A Study of Their Use in Conflict Settings*, Leiden 1971 [Brill], p. 448).

"Das Herz...ist die verborgene, inwendige Mitte und Wurzel des Menschen und damit seiner Welt...der unergründliche Grund und die lebendige Kraft aller Daseinserfahrung und—entscheidung" (H. Schlier, *Das Menschenherz nach dem Apostel Paulus*, in: *Lebendiges Zeugnis*, 1965, p. 123).

Cf. also F. Baumgärtel—J. Behm, "Kardia," in: *Theologisches Wörterbuch zum Neuen Testament*, II, Stuttgart 1933, (Kohlhammer), pp. 609-616.

3. This is perhaps the best-known one; but other similar examples can be found in the Bible (cf. Gn. 34:2; Jgs. 14:1, 16:1).

Lust Is the Fruit of the Breach of the Covenant with God

General audience of April 30, 1980.

1. During our last reflection, we said that the words of Christ in the Sermon on the Mount are in direct reference to the "lust" that arises immediately in the human heart; indirectly, however, those words guide us to understanding of a truth about man, which is of universal importance.

This truth about "historical" man, of universal importance, towards which the words of Christ, taken from Matthew 5:27-28, direct us, seems to be expressed in the biblical doctrine on the three forms of lust. We are referring here to the concise statement in the first letter of St. John 2:16-17: "For all that is in the world, the lust of the flesh and the lust of the eyes and the pride of life, is not of the Father but is of the world. And the world passes away, and the lust of it; but he who does the will of God abides forever."

It is obvious that to understand these words, it is necessary to take into careful consideration the context in which they appear, that is, the context of the whole "Johannine theology."[1] However, the same words are inserted, at the same time, in the context of the whole Bible: they belong to the whole revealed truth about man, and are important for the theology of the body. They do not explain lust itself in its threefold form, since they seem to assume that "the lust of the flesh and the lust of the eyes and the pride of life," are, in some way, a clear and known concept. They explain, however, the genesis of lust in its threefold form, indicating its origin which is "not of the Father," but "of the world."

2. The lust of the flesh and, together with it, the lust of the eyes and the pride of life, is "in the world" and at the same time "is of the world," not as the fruit of the mystery of creation, but as the fruit of the tree of knowledge of good and evil (cf. Gn. 2:17) in man's heart. What fructifies in the three forms of lust is not the "world" created by God for man, the fundamental "goodness" of which we have read several times in Genesis 1: "God saw that it was good...it was very good." In the three forms of lust there fructifies, on the contrary, the breaking of the first covenant with the Creator, with God-Elohim, with God-Yahweh. This covenant was broken in man's heart. It would be necessary to make here a careful analysis of the events described in Genesis 3:1-6. However, we are referring only in general to the mystery of sin, to the beginnings of human history. In fact, only as the consequence of sin, as the fruit of the breaking of the covenant with God in the

human heart—in the inner recesses of man—
has the "world" of the Book of Genesis become
the "world" of the Johannine words (1 Jn.
2:15-16): the place and source of lust.

In this way, therefore, the statement that
lust "is not of the Father but is of the world,"
seems to direct us once more to the biblical
"beginning." The genesis of lust in its three
forms, presented by John, finds in this beginning its first and fundamental elucidation, an
explanation, which is essential for the theology
of the body. To understand that truth of universal importance about "historical" man, contained in Christ's words during the Sermon on
the Mount (Mt. 5:27-28), we must return once
more to the Book of Genesis, and linger once
more "at the threshold" of the revelation of
"historical" man. That is all the more necessary, since this threshold of the history of
salvation proves to be at the same time the
threshold of authentic human experiences, as
we will see in the following analyses. The same
fundamental meanings, that we drew from the
preceding analyses, will come to life in them
again, as essential elements of a fitting anthropology and the deep substratum of the theology
of the body.

3. The question may arise again whether
it is permissible to transport the content typical of the "Johannine theology," contained in
the whole of the First Letter (particularly in
1 Jn. 2:15-16), to the ground of the Sermon on
the Mount according to Matthew, and precisely

of Christ's statement in Matthew 5:27-28 ("You have heard that it was said, You shall not commit adultery. But I say to you that everyone who looks at a woman lustfully has already committed adultery with her in his heart"). We will come back to this matter several times: nevertheless, we are referring straightaway to the general biblical context, to the whole of the truth about man, revealed and expressed in it. Precisely in the name of this truth, we are trying to understand completely the man that Christ indicates in the text of Matthew 5:27-28: that is, the man who "looks" at a woman "lustfully."

Is not this look, after all, to be explained by the fact that man is precisely a "man of lust," in the sense of the First Letter of St. John; in fact, that both of them, the man who looks lustfully and the woman who is the object of this look, are in the dimension of lust in its three forms, which "is not of the Father but is of the world"? It is necessary, therefore, to understand what that lust is or rather who is that "lustful man" of the Bible in order to discover the depths of Christ's words according to Matthew 5:27-28, and to explain the significance of their reference to the human "heart," so important for the theology of the body.

4. Let us return again to the Yahwist narrative, in which the same man, male and female, appears at the beginning as a man of original innocence—before original sin—and then as the one who lost innocence, by breaking the original covenant with his Creator. We do not

intend here to make a complete analysis of temptation and sin, according to the same text of Genesis 3:1-5, the doctrine of the Church in this connection and theology. It should merely be observed that the biblical description itself seems to highlight particularly the key moment, in which the Gift is questioned in man's heart. The man who gathers the fruit of the "tree of the knowledge of good and evil" makes, at the same time, a fundamental choice and carries it out against the will of the Creator, God-Yahweh, accepting the motivation suggested by the tempter: "You will not die. For God knows that when you eat of it your eyes will be opened, and you will be like God, knowing good and evil"; according to old translations: "you will be like gods, who know good and evil." [2]

This motivation clearly includes the questioning of the Gift and of the Love, from which creation has its origin as donation. As regards man, he receives the "world" as a gift and at the same time the "image of God" that is, humanity itself in all the truth of its male and female duality. It is enough to read carefully the whole passage of Genesis 3:1-5, to detect in it the mystery of man who turns his back on the "Father" (even if we do not find this name applied to God in the narrative). Questioning, in his heart, the deepest meaning of the donation, that is, love as the specific motive of the creation and of the original covenant (cf. in particular Gn. 3:5), man turns his back on God-Love, on "the Father." In a way he casts Him out of his heart. At the same time, therefore, he detaches his heart and almost cuts it off from what "is of the Father": thus, there remains in him what "is of the world."

5. "Then the eyes of both were opened, and they knew that they were naked; and they sewed fig leaves together and made themselves aprons" (Gn. 3:7). This is the first sentence of the Yahwist narrative, which refers to man's "situation" after sin and shows the new state of human nature. Does not this sentence also suggest the beginning of "lust" in man's heart? To answer this question more thoroughly, we cannot stop at that first sentence, but must read again the whole text. However, it is worth recalling here what was said in the first analyses on the subject of shame as the experience "of the limit."[3]

The Book of Genesis refers to this experience to show the "frontier" between the state of original innocence (cf. in particular Gn. 2:25, to which we devoted a great deal of attention in the preceding analyses) and man's sinfulness at the very "beginning." While Genesis 2:25 emphasizes that they "were both naked, and were not ashamed," Genesis 3:6 speaks explicitly of shame in connection with sin. That shame is almost the first source of the manifestation in man—in both, man and woman—of what "is not of the Father, but of the world."

FOOTNOTES

1. Cf. e.g.: J. Bonsirven, *Epitres de Saint Jean*, Paris 1954² (Beauchesne) pp. 113-119; E. Brooke, *Critical and*

Exegetical Commentary on the Johannine Epistles (International Critical Commentary), Edinburgh 1912 (Clark) pp. 47-49; P. De Ambroggi, *Le Epistole Cattoliche*, Torino 1947 (Marietti), pp. 216-217; C. H. Dodd, *The Johannine Epistles* (Moffatt New Testament Commentary), London 1946, pp. 41-42; J. Houlden, *A Commentary on the Johannine Epistles*, London 1973 (Black) pp. 73-74; B. Prete, *Lettere di Giovanni*, Roma 1970 (Ed. Paoline), p. 61; R. Schnackenburg, *Die Johannesbriefe*, Freiburg 1953 (Herders Theologischer Kommentar zum Neuen Testament) pp. 112-115; J. R. W. Stott, *Epistles of John* (Tyndale New Testament Commentaries) London 1969[3], pp. 99-101.

On the subject of John's theology, see in particular A. Feuillet, *Le mystère de l'amour divin dans la théologie johannique*, Paris 1972 (Gabalda).

2. The Hebrew text can have both meanings, because it runs: "ELOHIM knows that when you eat of it (the fruit of the tree of the knowledge of good and evil) your eyes will be opened, and you will be like ELOHIM, knowing good and evil." The term *elohim* is the plural of eloah ("pluralis excellentiae").

In relation to Yahweh, it has a singular meaning; but it may indicate the plural of other heavenly beings or pagan divinities (e.g. Ps. 8:6; Ex. 12:12; Jgs. 10:16; Hos. 31:1 and others).

Here are some translations:

—English: "you will be *like God*, knowing good and evil" (Revised Standard Version, 1966).

—French: "...vous serez *comme des dieux*, qui connaissent le bien et le mal (Bible de Jérusalem, 1973).

—Italian: "diverreste *come Dio*, conoscendo il bene e il male" (Pont. Istit. Biblico, 1961).

—Spanish: "seréis *como dioses*, conocedores del bien y del mal" (S. Ausejo Barcelona 1964).

"seréis *como Dios* en el conocimiento del bien y del mal." (A.-Alonso-Schokel, Madrid 1970).

3. Cf. General Audience of December 12, 1979 *(L'Osservatore Romano*, English edition, December 17, 1979).

Real Significance
of Original Nakedness

General audience of May 14, 1980.

1. We have already spoken of the shame which arose in the heart of the first man, male and female, together with sin. The first sentence of the biblical narrative, in this connection, runs as follows: "Then the eyes of both were opened, and they knew that they were naked; and they sewed fig leaves together and made themselves aprons" (Gn. 3:7). This passage, which speaks of the mutual shame of the man and the woman as a symptom of the fall *(status naturae lapsae)*, must be considered in its context. At that moment shame reaches its deepest level and seems to shake the very foundations of their existence. "And they heard the sound of the Lord God walking in the garden in the cool of the day, and the man and his wife hid themselves from the presence of the Lord God among the trees of the garden" (Gn. 3:8).

The necessity of hiding themselves indicates that in the depths of the shame they both feel before each other, as the immediate fruit of the tree of the knowledge of good and evil, there has matured a sense of fear before God: a fear previously unknown. The "Lord God called to the man, and said to him, 'Where are you?' And he said, 'I heard the sound of you in the garden, and I was afraid, because I was naked; and I hid myself'" (Gn. 3:9-10).

A certain fear always belongs to the very essence of shame; nevertheless original shame reveals its character in a particular way: "I was afraid, because I was naked." We realize that something deeper than physical shame, bound up with a recent consciousness of his own nakedness, is in action here. Man tries to cover with the shame of his own nakedness the real origin of fear, indicating rather its effect, in order not to call its cause by name. It is then that God-Yahweh says in His turn: "Who told you that you were naked? Have you eaten of the tree of which I commanded you not to eat?" (Gn. 3:11)

MAN ALIENATED FROM LOVE

2. The precision of that dialogue is overwhelming, the precision of the whole narrative is overwhelming. It manifests the surface of man's emotions in living the events, in such a way as to reveal at the same time their depth. In all this, "nakedness" has not solely a literal meaning, it does not refer only to the body, it is not the origin of a shame related only to the body. Actually, through "nakedness," there is manifested man deprived of participation in the Gift, man alienated from that Love which had

been the source of the original gift, the source of the fullness of the good intended for the creature.

This man, according to the formulas of the theological teaching of the Church,[1] was deprived of the supernatural and preternatural gifts which were part of his "endowment" before sin. Furthermore, he suffered a loss in what belongs to his nature itself, to humanity in the original fullness "of the image of God." The three forms of lust do not correspond to the fullness of that image, but precisely to the loss, the deficiencies, the limitations that appeared with sin.

Lust is explained as a lack, which, however, has its roots in the original depth of the human spirit. If we wish to study this phenomenon in its origins, that is, at the threshold of the experiences of "historical" man, we must take into consideration all the words that God-Yahweh addressed to the woman (Gn. 3:16) and to the man (Gn. 3:17-19), and furthermore, we must examine the state of their consciousness; and it is the Yahwist text that expressly enables us to do so. We have already called attention before to the literary specificity of the text in this connection.

A RADICAL CHANGE

3. What state of consciousness can be manifested in the words: "I was afraid, because I was naked; and I hid myself"? To what interior truth do they correspond? To what mean-

ing of the body do they testify? Certainly this new state differs a great deal from the original one. The words of Genesis 3:10 bear witness directly to a radical change of the meaning of original nakedness. In the state of original innocence, nakedness, as we pointed out previously, did not express a lack, but represented full acceptance of the body in all its human and therefore personal truth.

The body, as the expression of the person, was the first sign of man's presence in the visible world. In that world, man was able, right from the beginning, to distinguish himself, almost to be individualized—that is, confirm himself as a person—also through his own body. In fact, it had been marked, so to speak, as a visible factor of the transcendence in virtue of which man, as a person, surpasses the visible world of living beings *(animalia)*. In this sense, the human body was from the beginning a faithful witness and a tangible verification of man's original "solitude" in the world, becoming at the same time, by means of his masculinity and femininity, a limpid element of mutual donation in the communion of persons.

In this way, the human body bore in itself, in the mystery of creation, an unquestionable sign of the "image of God" and constituted also the specific source of the certainty of that image, present in the whole human being. Original acceptance of the body was, in a way, the basis of the acceptance of the whole visible world. And in its turn it was for man a guaran-

tee of his dominion over the world, over the
earth, which he was to subdue (cf. Gn. 1:28).

LOSS OF GOD'S IMAGE

4. The words "I was afraid, because I was
naked; and I hid myself" (Gn. 3:10), bear witness to a radical change in this relationship.
Man loses, in a way, the original certainty of the
"image of God," expressed in his body. He also
loses to some extent the sense of his right to
participate in the perception of the world, which
he enjoyed in the mystery of creation. This right
had its foundation in man's inner self, in the
fact that he himself participated in the divine
vision of the world and of his own humanity;
which gave him deep peace and joy in living the
truth and value of his own body, in all its
simplicity, transmitted to him by the Creator:
"God saw [that] it was very good" (Gn. 1:31).

The words of Genesis 3:10: "I was afraid,
because I was naked; and I hid myself," confirm
the collapse of the original acceptance of the
body as a sign of the person in the visible world.
At the same time, the acceptance of the material world in relation to man, also seems to be
shaken. The words of God-Yahweh are a forewarning, in a way, of the hostility of the world,
the resistance of nature with regard to man and
his tasks; they are a forewarning of the fatigue
that the human body was to feel in contact with
the earth subdued by him: "Cursed is the
ground because of you; in toil you shall eat of it
all the days of your life; thorns and thistles it

shall bring forth to you; and you shall eat the plants of the field. In the sweat of your face you shall eat bread till you return to the ground, for out of it you were taken" (Gn. 3:17-19). The end of this toil, of this struggle of man with the earth, is death: "You are dust, and to dust you shall return" (Gn. 3:19).

In this context, or rather in this perspective, Adam's words in Genesis 3:10: "I was afraid, because I was naked; and I hid myself," seem to express the awareness of being defenseless, and the sense of insecurity of his bodily structure before the processes of nature, operating with inevitable determinism. Perhaps, in this overwhelming statement there is implicit a certain "cosmic shame," in which the being created in "the image of God" and called to subdue the earth and dominate it (cf. Gn. 1:28) expresses himself precisely when, at the beginning of his historical experiences and in a manner so explicit, he is subjected to the earth, particularly in the "part" of his transcendent constitution represented precisely by the body.

FOOTNOTES

1. The Magisterium of the Church dealt more closely with these problems, in three periods, according to the needs of the age.

The declarations of the period of the controversies with the Pelagians (V-VI centuries) affirm that the first man, by

virtue of divine grace, possessed "naturalem possibilita-
tem et innocentiam" (DS 239), also called "freedom"
("libertas," "libertas arbitrii"), (DS 371, 242, 383, 622). He
remained in a state which the Synod of Orange (in the year
529) calls "integritas": "Natura humana, etiamsi *in illa
integritate, in qua condita est,* permaneret, nullo modo se
ipsam, Creatore suo non adiuvante, servaret..." (DS 389).

The concepts of "integritas" and, in particular, that
of "libertas," presuppose freedom from concupiscence,
although the ecclesiastical documents of this age do not
mention it explicitly.

The first man was furthermore free from the necessity
of death (DS 222, 372, 1511).

The Council of Trent defines the state of the first man,
prior to sin, as "holiness and justice" ("sanctitas et
iustitia"—DS 1511, 1512) or as "innocence" ("Innocentia"—DS 1521).

Further declarations on this matter defend the absolute
gratuitousness of the original gift of grace, against the
affirmations of the Jansenists. The "integritas primae crea-
tionis" was an unmerited elevation of human nature ("in-
debita humanae naturae exaltatio") and not "the state due
to him by nature" ("naturalis eius condicio"—DS 1926).
God, therefore, could have created man without these
graces and gifts (DS 1955); that would not have shattered
the essence of human nature and would not have deprived
it of its fundamental privileges (DS 1903-1907, 1909, 1921,
1923, 1924, 1926, 1955, 2434, 2437, 2616, 2617).

In analogy with the anti-Pelagian Synods, the Council
of Trent deals above all with the dogma of original sin,
integrating in its teaching preceding declarations in this
connection. Here, however, a certain clarification was intro-
duced, which partly changed the content comprised in the
concept of "liberum arbitrium." The "freedom" or "free
will" of the anti-Pelagian documents did not mean the
possibility of choice, connected with human nature, and
therefore constant, but referred only to the possibility of
carrying out meritorious acts, the freedom that springs
from grace and that man may lose.

Well, because of sin, Adam lost what did not belong to
human nature in the strict sense of the word, that is "integritas," "sanctitas," "innocentia," "iustitia." "Liberum
arbitrium," free will, was not taken away, but became
weaker:

"...liberum arbitrium minime exstinctum...viribus licet attenuatum et inclinatum..." (DS 1521—Trid. Sess. VI, Decr. de Justificatione, C. 1).

Together with sin appears concupiscence and the inevitability of death:

"...primum hominem...cum mandatum Dei...fuisset transgressus, statim sanctitatem et justitiam, in qua constitutus fuerat, amisisse *incurrisseque* per offensam praevaricationis huismodi iram et indignationem Dei atque ideo *mortem*...et cum morte captivitatem sub eius potestate, qui 'mortis' deinde 'habuit imperium'...'*totumque Adam per illam praevaricationis offensam secundum corpus et animam in deterius commutatum fuisse...*' " (DS 1511, Trid. Sess. V, Decr. de pecc. orig. 1).

(Cf. *Mysterium Salutis,* II, Einsiedeln-Zurich-Köln 1967, pp. 827-828: W. Seibel, "Der Mensch als Gottes übernatürliches Ebenbild und der Urstand des Menschen.")

A Fundamental Disquiet in All Human Existence

General audience of May 28, 1980.

1. We are reading again the first chapters of the Book of Genesis, to understand how—with original sin—the "man of lust" took the place of the "man of original innocence." The words of Genesis 3:10: "I was afraid, because I was naked; and I hid myself," which we considered two weeks ago, provide evidence of the first experience of man's shame with regard to his Creator: a shame that could also be called "cosmic."

However, this "cosmic shame"—if it is possible to perceive its features in man's total situation after original sin—makes way in the biblical text for another form of shame. It is the shame produced in humanity itself, caused by the deep disorder in that on account of which man, in the mystery of creation, was "God's image," both in his personal "ego" and in the interpersonal relationship, through the original communion of persons, constituted by the man and the woman together.

That shame, the cause of which is in humanity itself, is at once immanent and relative: it is manifested in the dimension of human interiority and at the same time refers to the "other." This is the woman's shame "with regard to" the man, and also the man's "with regard to" the woman: mutual shame, which obliges them to cover their own nakedness, to hide their own bodies, to remove from the man's sight what is the visible sign of femininity, and from the woman's sight what is the visible sign of masculinity.

The shame of both was turned in this direction after original sin, when they realized they "were naked," as Genesis 3:7 bears witness. The Yahwist text seems to indicate explicitly the "sexual" character of this shame: "they sewed fig leaves together and made themselves aprons." However, we may wonder if the "sexual" aspect has only a "relative" character; in other words: if it is a question of shame of one's own sexuality only in reference to a person of the other sex.

RELATIVE CHARACTER OF ORIGINAL SHAME

2. Although in the light of that one decisive sentence of Genesis 3:7, the answer to the question seems to support particularly the relative character of original shame, nevertheless reflection on the whole immediate context makes it possible to discover its more immanent background. That shame, which is certainly manifested in the "sexual" order, reveals a specific difficulty in perceiving the human

essentiality of one's own body: a difficulty
which man had not experienced in the state of
original innocence. In this way, in fact, the
words: "I was afraid, because I was naked," can
be understood; they show clearly the consequences of the fruit of the tree of the knowledge
of good and evil in man's heart.

Through these words there is revealed a
certain constitutive break within the human
person, almost a rupture of man's original
spiritual and somatic unity. He realizes for the
first time that his body has ceased drawing
upon the power of the spirit, which raised him
to the level of the image of God. His original
shame bears within it the signs of a specific
humiliation mediated by the body. There is concealed in it the germ of that contradiction,
which will accompany "historical" man in his
whole earthly path, as St. Paul writes: "For I
delight in the law of God, in my inmost self, but
I see in my members another law at war with
the law of my mind" (Rom. 7:22-23).

CENTER OF RESISTANCE

3. In this way, therefore, that shame is immanent. It contains such a cognitive acuteness
as to create a fundamental disquiet in the whole
of human existence, not only in face of the prospect of death, but also before that on which
there depend the value and dignity themselves
of the person in his ethical significance. In this
sense the original shame of the body ("I am

naked") is already fear ("I was afraid"), and announces the uneasiness of conscience connected with lust.

The body, which is not subordinated to the spirit as in the state of original innocence, bears within it a constant center of resistance to the spirit, and threatens, in a way, the unity of the man-person, that is, of the moral nature, which is firmly rooted in the very constitution of the person. Lust, and in particular the lust of the body, is a specific threat to the structure of self-control and self-mastery, through which the human person is formed. And it also constitutes a specific challenge for it. In any case, the man of lust does not control his own body in the same way, with equal simplicity and "naturalness," as the man of original innocence did. The structure of self-mastery, essential for the person, is, in a way, shaken to the very foundations in him; he again identifies himself with it in that he is continually ready to win it.

INTERIOR IMBALANCE

4. Immanent shame is connected with this interior imbalance. It has a "sexual" character, because the very sphere of human sexuality seems to highlight particularly that imbalance, which springs from lust and especially from the "lust of the body." From this point of view, that first impulse, of which Genesis 3:7 speaks ("they knew that they were naked; and they sewed fig leaves together and made themselves aprons") is very eloquent; it is as if the "man of

lust" (man and woman "in the act of knowledge of good and evil") felt that he had just stopped, also through his own body and sex, being above the world of living beings or "animalia." It is as if he felt a specific break of the personal integrity of his own body, particularly in what determines its sexuality and is directly connected with the call to that unity in which man and woman "become one flesh" (Gn. 2:24).

Therefore, that immanent and at the same time sexual shame is always, at least indirectly, relative. It is the shame of his own sexuality "with regard" to the other human being. In this way shame is manifested in the narrative of Genesis 3, as a result of which we are, .in a certain sense, witnesses of the birth of human lust. Also the motivation to go back from Christ's words about man (male), who "looks at a woman lustfully" (Mt. 5:27-28), to that first moment in which shame is explained by means of lust, and lust by means of shame, is therefore sufficiently clear. In this way we understand better why—and in what sense—Christ speaks of desire as "adultery" committed in the heart, because He addresses the human "heart."

DESIRE AND SHAME

5. The human heart keeps within it simultaneously desire and shame. The birth of shame directs us towards that moment in which the inner man, "the heart," closing himself to what "comes from the Father," opens to what "comes

from the world." The birth of shame in the human heart keeps pace with the beginning of lust—of the threefold concupiscence according to Johannine theology (cf. 1 Jn. 2:16), and in particular the concupiscence of the body.

Man is ashamed of his body because of lust. In fact, he is ashamed not so much of his body as precisely of lust: he is ashamed of his body owing to lust. He is ashamed of his body owing to that state of his spirit to which theology and psychology give the same synonymic denomination: desire or lust, although with a meaning that is not quite the same.

The biblical and theological meaning of desire and lust is different from that used in psychology. For the latter, desire comes from lack or necessity, which the value desired must satisfy. Biblical lust, as we can deduce from 1 Jn. 2:16, indicates the state of the human spirit removed from the original simplicity and the fullness of values that man and the world possess "in the dimensions of God." Precisely this simplicity and fullness of the value of the human body in the first experience of its masculinity-femininity, of which Genesis 2:23-25 speaks, has subsequently undergone, "in the dimensions of the world," a radical transformation. And then, together with the lust of the body, shame was born.

DOUBLE MEANING

6. Shame has a double meaning: it indicates the threat to the value and at the same time preserves this value interiorly.[1] The fact

that the human heart, from the moment when the lust of the body was born in it keeps also shame within itself, indicates that it is possible and necessary to appeal to it when it is a question of guaranteeing those values from which lust takes away their original and full dimension. If we keep that in mind, we are able to understand better why Christ, speaking of lust, appeals to the human "heart."

FOOTNOTES

1. Cf. Karol Wojtyla, *Amore e responsabilita*, Turin 1978, chap. "Metafisica del pudore," pp. 161-178.

Relationship of Lust
to Communion of Persons

General audience of June 4, 1980.

1. Speaking of the birth of man's lust, on the basis of the Book of Genesis, we analyzed the original meaning of shame, which appeared with the first sin. The analysis of shame, in the light of the biblical narrative, enables us to understand even more thoroughly the meaning it has for interpersonal man-woman relations as a whole. The third chapter of Genesis shows without any doubt that that shame appeared in man's mutual relationship with woman and that this relationship, by reason of the very shame itself, underwent a radical transformation. Since it was born in their hearts together with the lust of the body, the analysis of original shame enables us at the same time to examine in what relationship this lust remains with regard to the communion of persons, which was granted and assigned from the beginning as the man and woman's task owing to the fact that they had been created "in the image of God." Therefore, the further stage of the study of lust, which had been manifested "at the beginning" through the man and woman's shame, accord-

ing to Genesis 3, is the analysis of the insatiability of the union, that is, of the communion of persons, which was to be expressed also by their bodies, according to their specific masculinity and femininity.

CHANGES IN MAN-WOMAN RELATIONSHIP

2. Above all, therefore, this shame, which, according to the biblical narrative, induces man and woman to hide from each other their bodies and particularly their sexual differentiation, confirms that the original capacity of communicating themselves to each other, of which Genesis 2:25 speaks, has been shattered. The radical change of the meaning of original nakedness leads us to presume negative changes in the whole interpersonal man-woman relationship. That mutual communion in humanity itself by means of the body and by means of its masculinity and femininity, which resounded so strongly in the preceding passage of the Yahwist narrative (cf. Gn. 2:23-25), is upset at this moment: as if the body, in its masculinity and femininity, no longer constituted the "trustworthy" substratum of the communion of persons, as if its original function were "called in question" in the consciousness of man and woman.

The simplicity and "purity" of the original experience, which facilitated an extraordinary fullness in the mutual communication of each other, disappear. Obviously, our first progenitors did not stop communicating with each other through the body and its movements, gestures and expressions; but the simple and direct communion with each other, connected with the original experience of reciprocal nakedness, disappeared. Almost unexpectedly, there appeared in their consciousness an insuperable threshold, which limited the original "giving of oneself" to the other, in full confidence in what constituted their own identity and, at the same time, their diversity, female on the one side, male on the other. The diversity, that is, the difference of the male sex and the female sex, was suddenly felt and understood as an element of mutual confrontation of persons. This is testified to by the concise expression of Genesis 3:7, "They knew that they were naked," and by its immediate context. All that is part also of the analysis of the first shame. The Book of Genesis not only portrays its origin in the human being, but makes it possible also to reveal its degrees in both, man and woman.

LOSS OF THAT ORIGINAL CERTAINTY

3. The ending of the capacity of a full mutual communion, which is manifested as sexual shame, enables us to understand better the original value of the unifying meaning of the body. It is not possible, in fact, to understand otherwise that respective closure to each other, or shame, unless in relation to the meaning that

the body, in its femininity and masculinity, had for man previously, in the state of original innocence. That unifying meaning is understood not only with regard to the unity that man and woman, as spouses, were to constitute, becoming "one flesh" (Gn. 2:24) through the conjugal act, but also in reference to the "communion of persons" itself, which had been the specific dimension of man and woman's existence in the mystery of creation. The body in its masculinity and femininity constituted the peculiar "substratum" of this personal communion. Sexual shame, with which Genesis 3:7 deals, bears witness to the loss of the original certainty that the human body, through its masculinity and femininity, is precisely that "substratum" of the communion of persons, that expresses it "simply," that it serves the purpose of realizing it (and thus also of completing the "image of God" in the visible world).

This state of consciousness in both has strong repercussions in the further context of Genesis 3, with which we shall deal shortly. If man, after original sin, had lost, so to speak, the sense of the image of God in himself, that loss was manifested with shame of the body (cf. particularly Gn. 3:10-11). That shame, encroaching upon the man-woman relationship in its totality, was manifested with the imbalance of the original meaning of corporeal unity, that is, of the body as the peculiar "substratum" of the communion of persons. As if the personal profile of masculinity and femininity, which, before, highlighted the meaning of the body for a full communion of persons, had made way only for the sensation of "sexuality" with regard to the other human being. And as if sexuality became an "obstacle" in the personal relationship of man and woman. Concealing it from each other, according to Genesis 3:7, they both express it almost instinctively.

SECOND DISCOVERY OF SEX

4. This is, at the same time, the "second" discovery of sex, as it were, which in the biblical narrative differs radically from the first one. The whole context of the narrative confirms that this new discovery distinguishes "historical" man with his lust (with the three forms of lust, in fact) from man of original innocence. What is the relationship of lust, and in particular the lust of the flesh, with regard to the communion of persons mediated by the body, by its masculinity and femininity, that is, to the communion assigned, "from the beginning" to man by the Creator? This is the question that must be posed, precisely with regard "to the beginning," about the experience of shame, to which the biblical narrative refers.

Shame, as we have already observed, is manifested in the narrative of Genesis 3 as a symptom of man's detachment from the love in which he participated in the mystery of creation according to the Johannine expression: the love that "comes from the Father." "The love that is in the world," that is, lust, brings with it an almost constitutive difficulty of identification with one's own body: and not only in the sphere of one's own subjectivity, but even more with regard to the subjectivity of the other human being: of woman for man, of man for woman.

COLLAPSE OF ORIGINAL COMMUNION

5. Hence the necessity of hiding before the "other" with one's own body, with what determines one's own femininity-masculinity. This necessity proves the fundamental lack of trust, which in itself indicates the collapse of the original relationship "of communion." Precisely regard for the subjectivity of the other, and at the same time for one's own subjectivity, has aroused in this new situation, that is, in the context of lust, the necessity of hiding oneself, of which Genesis 3:7 speaks.

Precisely here it seems to us that we can discover a deeper meaning of "sexual" shame and also the full meaning of that phenomenon, to which the biblical text refers, to point out the boundary between the man of original innocence and the "historical" man of lust. The complete text of Genesis 3 supplies us with elements to define the deepest dimension of shame; but that calls for a separate analysis. We will begin it in the next reflection.

Dominion over the Other
in the Interpersonal Relation

General audience of June 18, 1980.

1. The phenomenon of shame, which appeared in the first man together with original sin, is described with surprising precision in Genesis 3. Careful reflection on this text enables us to deduce from it that shame, which took the place of the absolute trust connected with the previous state of original innocence in the mutual relationship between man and woman, has a deeper dimension. In this connection it is necessary to reread chapter 3 of Genesis to the end, and not limit ourselves to verse 7 or the text of verses 10-11, which contain the testimony about the first experience of shame. After this narrative, the dialogue of God-Yahweh with the man and the woman breaks off and a monologue begins. Yahweh turns to the woman and speaks first of the pain of childbirth, which will accompany her from now on: "I will greatly multiply your pain in childbearing; in pain you shall bring forth children..." (Gn. 3:16).

That is followed by the expression which characterizes the future relationship of both, of

the man and the woman: "your desire shall be
for your husband, and he shall rule over you"
(Gn. 3:16).

A PARTICULAR "DISABILITY"
OF WOMAN

2. These words, like those of Genesis 2:24,
have a perspective character. The incisive formulation of 3:16 seems to regard the facts as a
whole, which have already emerged, in a way,
in the original experience of shame, and which
will subsequently be manifested in the whole
interior experience of "historical" man. The
history of consciences and of human hearts will
contain the continual confirmation of the words
contained in Genesis 3:16. The words spoken at
the beginning seem to refer to a particular "disability" of woman as compared with man. But
there is no reason to understand it as a social
disability or inequality. The expression: "your
desire shall be for your husband, and he shall
rule over you" immediately indicate, on the
other hand, another form of inequality, which
woman will feel as a lack of full unity precisely
in the vast context of union with man, to which
both were called according to Genesis 2:24.

A FUNDAMENTAL LOSS

3. The words of God-Yahweh: "your desire
shall be for your husband, and he shall rule over
you" (Gn. 3:16), do not concern exclusively the
moment of man and woman's union, when

both unite in such a way as to become one flesh (cf. Gn. 2:24), but refer to the ample context of relations, also indirect ones, of conjugal union as a whole. For the first time the man is defined here as "husband." In the whole context of the Yahwist narrative these words mean above all, a violation, a fundamental loss, of the original community-communion of persons. The latter should have made man and woman mutually happy by means of the pursuit of a simple and pure union in humanity, by means of a reciprocal offering of themselves, that is, the experience of the gift of the person expressed with the soul and with the body, with masculinity and femininity ("flesh of my flesh": Gn. 2:23), and finally by means of the subordination of this union to the blessing of fertility with "procreation."

DISTORTED BY LUST

4. It seems, therefore, that in the words addressed by God-Yahweh to the woman, there is a deeper echo of the shame, which they both began to experience after the breaking of the original covenant with God. We find, moreover, a fuller motivation of this shame. In a very discreet way, which is, nevertheless, decipherable and expressive, Genesis 3:16 testifies how that original beatifying conjugal union of persons will be distorted in man's heart by lust. These words are addressed directly to woman, but they refer to man, or rather to both together.

DOMINION OVER WOMAN

5. The previous analysis of Genesis 3:7 already showed that in the new situation, after the breaking of the original covenant with God, the man and the woman found themselves, instead of united, more divided or even opposed because of their masculinity and femininity. The biblical narrative, stressing the instinctive impulse that had driven them both to cover their bodies, describes at the same time the situation in which man, as male *or* female —before it was rather male *and* female—feels more estranged from the body, as from the source of the original union in humanity ("flesh of my flesh"), and more opposed to the other precisely on the basis of the body and sex. This opposition does not destroy or exclude conjugal union, willed by the Creator (cf. Gn. 2:24), or its procreative effects; but it confers on the realization of this union another direction, which will be precisely that of the man of lust. Genesis 3:16 speaks precisely of this.

The woman, whose "desire shall be for (her) husband" (cf. Gn. 3:16), and the man who responds to this desire, as we read: "shall rule over you," unquestionably form the same human couple, the same marriage as Genesis 2:24, in fact, the same community of persons; however, they are now something different. They are no longer called only to union and unity, but also threatened by the insatiability of that union and unity, which does not cease to attract man and woman precisely because they are persons, called from eternity to exist "in communion." In the light of the biblical narrative, sexual shame has its deep meaning, which is connected precisely with the failure to satisfy the aspiration to realize in the "conjugal union of the body" (cf. Gn. 2:24) the mutual communion of persons.

THREEFOLD LUST

6. All that seems to confirm, from various aspects, that at the basis of shame, in which "historical" man has become a participant, there is the threefold lust spoken of in the First Letter of John 2:16: not only the lust of the flesh, but also "the lust of the eyes and the pride of life." Does not the expression regarding "rule" ("he shall rule over you"), of which we read in Genesis 3:16, indicate this last form of lust? Does not the rule "over" the other—of man over woman—change essentially the structure of communion in the interpersonal relationship? Does it not transpose into the dimension of this structure something 'that makes the human being an object, which can, in a way, be desired by the lust of the eyes?

These are the questions that spring from reflection on the words of God-Yahweh according to Genesis 3:16. Those words, delivered almost on the threshold of human history after original sin, reveal to us not only the exterior situation of man and woman, but enable us also to penetrate into the deep mysteries of their hearts.

Lust Limits Nuptial Meaning of the Body

General audience of June 25, 1980.

1. The analysis we made during the preceding reflection was centered on the following words of Genesis 3:16, addressed by God-Yahweh to the first woman after original sin: "your desire shall be for your husband, and he shall rule over you" (Gn. 3:16). We arrived at the conclusion that these words contain an adequate clarification and a deep interpretation of original shame (cf. Gn. 3:7), which became part of man and of woman together with lust. The explanation of this shame is not to be sought in the body itself, in the somatic sexuality of both, but goes back to the deeper changes undergone by the human spirit. Precisely this spirit is particularly aware of how insatiable it is with regard to the mutual unity between man and woman.

This awareness, so to speak, blames the body, and deprives it of the simplicity and purity of the meaning connected with the original innocence of the human being. In relation to this awareness, shame is a secondary experience. If on the one hand it reveals the moment of lust, at the same time it can protect from the consequences of the three forms of lust. It can even be said that man and woman, through shame, almost remain in the state of original innocence. Continually, in fact, they become aware of the nuptial meaning of the body and aim at preserving it, so to speak, from lust, just as they try to maintain the value of communion, that is, of the union of persons in the "unity of the body."

BETTER UNDERSTANDING

2. Genesis 2:24 speaks with discretion but also with clarity of the "union of bodies" in the sense of the authentic union of persons: "A man...cleaves to his wife, and they become one flesh"; and it is seen from the context that this union comes from a choice, since the man "leaves" his father and mother to unite with his wife. Such a union of persons entails that they should become "one flesh." Starting from this "sacramental" expression, which corresponds to the communion of persons—of the man and the woman—in their original call to conjugal union, we can understand better the specific message of Genesis 3:16; that is, we can establish and, as it were, reconstruct what the imbalance, in fact, the peculiar distortion of the original interpersonal relationship of communion, to which the "sacramental" words of Genesis 2:24 refer, consists of.

IMPULSE TO DOMINATE

3. It can therefore be said—studying Genesis 3:16—that while on the one hand the

"body," constituted in the unity of the personal subject, does not cease to stimulate the desires of personal union, precisely because of masculinity and femininity ("your desire shall be for your husband"), on the other hand and at the same time, lust directs these desires in its own way. That is confirmed by the expression: "he shall rule over you."

The lust of the flesh directs these desires, however, to satisfaction of the body, often at the cost of a real and full communion of persons. In this sense, attention should be paid to the way in which semantic accentuations are distributed in the verses of Genesis 3; in fact, although there are few of them, they reveal interior consistency. The man is the one who seems to feel ashamed of his own body with particular intensity: "I was afraid, because I was naked; and I hid myself" (Gn. 3:10). These words emphasize the really metaphysical character of shame. At the same time, the man is the one for whom shame, united with lust, will become an impulse to "dominate" the woman ("he shall rule over you").

Subsequently, the experience of this domination is manifested more directly in the woman as the insatiable desire for a different union. From the moment when the man "dominates" her, the communion of persons—made of the full spiritual union of the two subjects giving themselves to each other—is followed by a different mutual relationship, that is, the relationship of possession of the other as the object of one's own desire. If this impulse prevails on the part of the man, the instincts that the woman directs to him, according to the expression of Genesis 3:16, can—and do—assume a similar character. And sometimes, perhaps, they precede the man's "desire," or even aim at arousing it and giving it impetus.

AN INTERIOR DIMENSION

4. The text of Genesis 3:16 seems to indicate the man particularly as the one who "desires," similarly to the text of Matthew 5:27-28, which is the starting point of these meditations. Nevertheless, both the man and the woman have become a "human being" subject to lust. And therefore the lot of both is shame, which with its deep resonance touches the innermost recesses both of the male and of the female personality, even though in a different way. What we learn from Genesis 3 enables us barely to outline this duality, but even the mere references are already very significant. Let us add that, since it is a question of such an archaic text, it is surprisingly eloquent and acute.

SIMILAR EXPERIENCES

5. An adequate analysis of Genesis 3 leads therefore to the conclusion that the three forms of lust, including that of the body, bring with them a limitation of the nuptial meaning of the body itself, in which man and woman partici-

pated in the state of original innocence. When we speak of the meaning of the body, we refer in the first place to the full awareness of the human being, but we also include all actual experience of the body in its masculinity and femininity, and, in any case, the constant predisposition to this experience.

The "meaning" of the body is not just something conceptual. We have already drawn attention to this sufficiently in the preceding analyses. The "meaning of the body" is at the same time what determines the attitude: it is the way of living the body. It is a measure which the interior man, that is, that "heart" to which Christ refers in the Sermon on the Mount, applies to the human body with regard to his masculinity/femininity (therefore with regard to his sexuality).

That "meaning" does not change the reality in itself, that which the human body is and does not cease to be in the sexuality that is characteristic of it, independently of the states of our conscience and our experiences. However, this purely objective significance of the body and of sex, outside the system of real and concrete interpersonal relations between man and woman, is, in a certain sense, "a-historical." In the present analysis, on the contrary—in conformity with the biblical sources—we always take man's historicity into account (also because of the fact that we start from his theological prehistory). It is a question here, obviously, of an interior dimension, which eludes the external criteria of historicity, but which, however, can be considered "historical." In fact, it is precisely at the basis of all the facts which constitute the history of man—also the history of sin and of salvation—and thus reveal the depth and very root of his historicity.

LINKED WITH
THE SERMON ON THE MOUNT

6. When, in this vast context, we speak of lust as limitation, infraction or even distortion of the nuptial meaning of the body, we are referring above all to the preceding analyses regarding the state of original innocence, that is, the theological prehistory of man. At the same time, we have in mind the measure that "historical" man, with his "heart," applies to his own body in relation to male/female sexuality. This measure is not something exclusively conceptual: it is what determines the attitudes and decides in general the way of living the body.

Certainly, Christ refers to that in His Sermon on the Mount. We are trying here to link up the words taken from Matthew 5:27-28 to the very threshold of man's theological history, taking them, therefore, into consideration already in the context of Genesis 3. Lust as limitation, infraction or even distortion of the nuptial meaning of the body can be ascertained in a particularly clear way (in spite of the concise nature of the biblical narrative) in our first progenitors, Adam and Eve. Thanks to them we have been able to find the nuptial meaning of the body and rediscover what it consists of as a measure of the human "heart," such as to mold the original form of the communion of persons. If in their personal experience (which the biblical text enables us to follow) that original form *has undergone imbalance and distortion*—as we have sought to prove through the analysis of shame—*also the nuptial meaning of the body, which in the situation of original innocence constituted the measure of the heart of both, of the man and of the woman, must have undergone a distortion.* If we succeed in reconstructing in what this distortion consists, we shall also have the answer to our question: that is, what lust of the flesh consists of and what constitutes its theological and at the same time anthropological specific character. It seems that an answer theologically and anthropologically adequate—important as regards the meaning of Christ's words in the Sermon on the Mount (Mt. 5:27-28)—can already be obtained from the context of Genesis 3 and from the whole Yahwist narrative, which previously enabled us to clarify the nuptial meaning of the human body.

The "Heart"— a Battlefield Between Love and Lust

General audience of July 23, 1980.

1. The human body in its original masculinity and femininity according to the mystery of creation—as we know from the analysis of Genesis 2:23-25—is not only a source of fertility, that is, of procreation, but right "from the beginning" has a nuptial character: that is to say, it is capable of expressing the love with which the man-person becomes a gift, thus fulfilling the deep meaning of his being and his existence. In this peculiarity, the body is the expression of the spirit and is called, in the very mystery of creation, to exist in the communion of persons "in the image of God." Well, the concupiscence "that comes from the world" —here it is directly a question of the concupiscence of the body—limits and distorts the body's objective way of existing, of which man has become a participant.

The human "heart" experiences the degree of this limitation or distortion, especially in the sphere of man-woman mutual relations. Precisely in the experience of the "heart" femininity and masculinity, in their mutual relations, no longer seem to be the expression of the spirit which aims at personal communion, and remain only an object of attraction, in a certain sense as happens "in the world" of living beings, which, like man, have received the blessing of fertility (cf. Gn. 1).

2. This similarity is certainly contained in the work of creation; also Genesis 2 and particularly verse 24 confirm this. However, already in the mystery of creation, that which constituted the "natural," somatic and sexual substratum of that attraction, fully expressed the call of man and woman to personal communion. After sin, on the contrary, in the new situation of which Genesis 3 speaks, this expression was weakened and dimmed: as if it were lacking in the shaping of mutual relations, or as if it were driven back to another plane.

The natural and somatic substratum of human sexuality was manifested as an almost autogenous force, marked by a certain "coercion of the body," operating according to its own dynamics, which limits the expression of the spirit and the experience of the exchange of the gift of the person. The words of Genesis 3:15 addressed to the first woman seem to indicate this quite clearly ("your desire shall be for your husband, and he shall rule over you").

3. The human body in its masculinity/femininity has almost lost the capacity of expressing this love, in which the man-person

becomes a gift, in conformity with the deepest structure and finality of his personal existence, as we have already observed in preceding analyses. If here we do not formulate this judgment absolutely and add the adverbial expression "almost," we do so because the dimension of the gift—namely, the capacity of expressing love with which man, by means of femininity or masculinity, becomes a gift for the other—has continued to some extent to permeate and mold the love that is born in the human heart. The nuptial meaning of the body has not become completely suffocated by concupiscence, but only habitually threatened.

The "heart" has become a battlefield between love and lust. The more lust dominates the heart, the less the latter experiences the nuptial meaning of the body, and the less it becomes sensitive to the gift of the person, which, in the mutual relations of man and of woman expresses precisely that meaning. Certainly, that "lust" also of which Christ speaks in Matthew 5:27-28, appears in many forms in the human heart: it is not always plain and obvious; sometimes it is concealed, so that it passes itself off as "love," although it changes its true profile and dims the limpidity of the gift in the mutual relationship of persons. Does this mean that it is our duty to distrust the human heart? No! It only means that we must keep it under control.

4. The image of the concupiscence of the body, which emerges from the present analysis,

has a clear reference to the image of the person, with which we connected our preceding reflections on the subject of the nuptial meaning of the body. Man, indeed, as a person is "the only creature on earth that God has willed for its own sake" and, at the same time, he is the one who "can fully discover his true self only in a sincere giving of himself." [1] Lust in general—and the lust of the body in particular—attacks precisely this "sincere giving." It deprives man, it could be said, of the dignity of giving, which is expressed by his body through femininity and masculinity, and in a way it "depersonalizes" man making him an object "for the other." Instead of being "together with the other"—a subject in unity, in fact, in the sacramental unity "of the body"—man becomes an object for man: the female for the male and vice versa. The words of Genesis 3:16—and, even before, of Genesis 3:7—bear witness to this, with all the clearness of the contrast, as compared with Genesis 2:23-25.

5. Violating the dimension of the mutual giving of the man and the woman, concupiscence also calls in question the fact that each of them was willed by the Creator "for his own sake." The subjectivity of the person gives way, in a certain sense, to the objectivity of the body. Owing to the body, man becomes an object for man—the female for the male and vice versa. Concupiscence means, so to speak, that the personal relations of man and of woman are unilaterally and reductively linked with the

body and sex, in the sense that these relations become almost incapable of accepting the mutual gift of the person. They do not contain or deal with femininity/masculinity according to the full dimension of personal subjectivity; they are not the expression of communion, but they remain unilaterally determined "by sex."

6. Concupiscence entails the loss of the interior freedom of the gift. The nuptial meaning of the human body is connected precisely with this freedom. Man can become a gift—that is, the man and the woman can exist in the relationship of mutual self-giving, if each of them controls himself. Concupiscence, which is manifested as a "coercion *sui generis* of the body," limits interiorly and reduces self-control, and for that reason, makes impossible, in a certain sense, the interior freedom of giving. Together with that, also the beauty that the human body possesses in its male and female aspect, as an expression of the spirit, is obscured. There remains the body as an object of lust and, therefore, as a "field of appropriation" of the other human being. Concupiscence, in itself, is not capable of promoting union as the communion of persons. By itself, it does not unite, but appropriates. The relationship of the gift is changed into the relationship of appropriation.

At this point, let us interrupt our reflections today. The last problem dealt with here is of such great importance, and is, moreover, so subtle, from the point of view of the difference between authentic love (that is, between the "communion of persons") and lust, that we shall have to take it up again at our next meeting.

FOOTNOTES

1. *Gaudium et spes,* no. 24: "Furthermore, the Lord Jesus, when praying to the Father 'that they may all be one...even as we are one' (Jn. 17:21-22), has opened up new horizons closed to human reason by implying that there is a certain parallel between the union existing among the Divine Persons and the union of the sons of God in truth and love. It follows, then, that if man is the only creature on earth that God has willed for its own sake, man can fully discover his true self only in a sincere giving of himself."

Opposition in the Human Heart Between the Spirit and the Body

General audience of July 30, 1980.

1. The reflections we are developing in the present cycle refer to the words which Christ uttered in the Sermon on the Mount on man's "lust" for woman. In the attempt to proceed with a thorough examination of what characterizes the "man of lust," we went back again to the Book of Genesis. Here, the situation that came into being in the mutual relationship of man and woman is portrayed with great delicacy. The single sentences of Genesis 3 are very eloquent. The words of God-Yahweh addressed to woman in Genesis 3:16: "Your desire shall be for your husband, and he shall rule over you," seem to reveal, upon a careful analysis, in what way the relationship of mutual giving, which existed between them in the state of original innocence, changed after original sin to a relationship of mutual appropriation.

If man in his relationship with woman considers her only as an object to gain possession of and not as a gift, he condemns himself thereby to become also for her only an object of appropriation, and not a gift. It seems that the words of Genesis 3:16 deal with this bilateral relationship, although the only thing they say directly is: "he shall rule over you." Furthermore, in unilateral appropriation (which indirectly is bilateral) the structure of communion between persons disappears. Both human beings become almost incapable of attaining the interior measure of the heart, directed to the freedom of the giving of oneself and the nuptial meaning of the body, which is intrinsic to it. The words of Genesis 3:16 seem to suggest that it is often at the expense of the woman that this happens, and that in any case she feels it more than man.

2. It is worth turning our attention now to this detail at least. The words of God-Yahweh according to Genesis 3:16: "Your desire shall be for your husband, and he shall rule over you," and those of Christ according to Matthew 5:27-28: "Everyone who looks at a woman lustfully....," make it possible to perceive a certain parallelism. Perhaps it is not a question here of the fact that the woman particularly becomes the object of man's "lust," but rather that—as we have already stressed previously— "from the beginning" man was to have been the guardian of the reciprocity of donation and its true balance.

The analysis of that "beginning" (Gn. 2:23-25) shows precisely man's responsibility in accepting femininity as a gift and in borrowing it in a mutual, bilateral exchange. To take from woman her own gift by means of concupiscence, is in open contrast with that. Although the maintenance of the balance of the gift seems to have been entrusted to both, a special responsibility rests with man above all, as if it depended more on him whether the balance is maintained or broken or even—if already broken—re-established.

Certainly, the diversity of roles according to these statements, to which we are referring here as to key-texts, was also dictated by the social emargination of woman in the conditions of that time (and the Holy Scripture of the Old and the New Testament gives us sufficient proofs of this); nevertheless, it contains a truth, which has its weight independently of specific conditionings due to the customs of that given historical situation.

3. As a consequence of lust, the body becomes almost a "ground" of appropriation of the other person. As is easy to understand, that entails the loss of the nuptial meaning of the body. And together with that also the mutual "belonging" of persons, who, uniting so as to "become one flesh" (Gn. 2:24), are called at the same time to belong to each other, acquires another meaning. The particular dimension of the personal union of man and woman through love is expressed in the word "my." This pronoun, which has always belonged to the language of human love, often recurs in the verses of the Song of Songs and also in other biblical texts.[1] It is a pronoun which, in its "material" meaning, denotes a relationship of

possession, but in our case indicates the personal analogy of this relationship.

The mutual belonging of man and woman, especially when they belong to each other as spouses "in unity of the body," is formed according to this personal analogy. An analogy—as is well known—indicates, at the same time, similarity and also the lack of identity (namely, a substantial dissimilarity). We can speak of persons belonging to each other only if we take such an analogy into consideration. In fact, in its original and specific meaning, belonging presupposes the relationship of the subject to the object: a relationship of possession and ownership. It is a relationship that is not only objective, but above all "material": the belonging of something, and therefore of an object to someone.

4. In the eternal language of human love, the term "my" certainly does not have this meaning. It indicates the reciprocity of the donation, it expresses the equal balance of the gift—precisely this, perhaps, in the first place —namely, that balance of the gift in which the mutual *communio personarum* is established. And if this is established by means of the mutual gift of masculinity and femininity, there is also preserved in it the nuptial meaning of the body.

In the language of love, in fact, the word "my" seems a radical negation of belonging in the sense in which an object-thing belongs to the subject-person. The analogy preserves its functions until it falls into the meaning set forth above. Triple lust, and in particular the lust of the flesh, takes away from the mutual belonging of man and woman the specific dimension of the personal analogy, in which the term "my" preserves its essential meaning. This essential meaning lies outside the "law of ownership," outside the meaning of "object of possession"; concupiscence, on the contrary, is directed towards the latter meaning.

From possessing, a further step goes towards "enjoyment": the object I possess acquires a certain meaning for me since it is at my disposal and I avail myself of it, I use it. It is evident that the personal analogy of belonging is decidedly opposed to this meaning. And this opposition is a sign that what, in the mutual relationship of man and woman, "comes from the Father," still persists and continues in confrontation with what comes "from the world." However, concupiscence in itself drives man towards possession of the other as an object, drives him to "enjoyment," which brings with it the negation of the nuptial meaning of the body. In its essence, disinterested giving is excluded from selfish "enjoyment." Do not the words of God-Yahweh addressed to woman in Genesis 3:16 already speak of this?

5. According to the First Letter of John (2:16), lust bears witness in the first place to the state of the human spirit. It will be opportune to devote a further analysis to this problem. Applying Johannine theology to the field of the ex-

periences described in Genesis 3, as well as to the words spoken by Christ in the Sermon on the Mount (Mt. 5:27-28), we find, so to speak, a concrete dimension of that opposition which —together with sin—was born in the human heart between the spirit and the body.

Its consequences are felt in the mutual relationship of persons, whose unity in humanity is determined right from the beginning by the fact that they are man and woman. Since "another law at war with the law of (my) mind" (Rom. 7:23) has been installed in man, there exists almost a constant danger of this way of seeing, evaluating, and loving, so that "the desire of the body" is more powerful than "the desire of the mind." And it is precisely this truth about man, this anthropological element that we must always keep in mind, if we wish to understand completely the appeal made by Christ to the human heart in the Sermon on the Mount.

FOOTNOTES

1. Cf., for example, Song of Songs, 1:9, 13, 14, 15, 16; 2:2, 3, 8, 9, 10, 13, 14, 16, 17; 3:2, 4, 5; 4:1, 10; 5:1, 2, 4; 6:2, 3, 4, 9; 7:11; 8:12, 14.
   Cf. also, for example, Ez. 16:8; Hos. 2:18; Tb. 8:7.

Sermon on the Mount to the Men of Our Day

General audience of August 6, 1980.

1. Continuing our cycle, let us take up again today the Sermon on the Mount, and precisely the statement: "Everyone who looks at a woman lustfully has already committed adultery with her in his heart" (Mt. 5:28). Jesus appeals here to the "heart."

In his talk with the Pharisees, Jesus, referring to the "beginning" (cf. the preceding analyses), uttered the following words with regard to the certificate of divorce: "For your hardness of heart Moses allowed you to divorce your wives, but from the beginning it was not so" (Mt. 19:8). This sentence undoubtedly contains an accusation. "Hardness of heart"[1] indicates what, according to the ethos of the people of the Old Testament, had brought about the situation contrary to the original plan of God-Yahweh according to Genesis 2:24. And it is there that the key must be sought to interpret the whole legislation of Israel in the sphere of marriage and, in the wider sense, in relations between man and woman as a whole. Speaking of "hardness of heart," Christ accuses, so to speak, the whole "interior subject" who is responsible for the distortion of the law. In the Sermon on the Mount (Mt. 5:27-28), He also refers to the "heart," but the words pronounced here do not seem only to accuse.

2. We must reflect on them once more, placing them as far as possible in their "historical" dimension. The analysis made so far—aimed at highlighting "the man of lust" in his genetic moment, almost at the initial point of his history interwoven with theology—constitutes an ample introduction, particularly an anthropological one, to the work that must still be undertaken. The following stage of our analysis will have to be of an ethical character.

The Sermon on the Mount, and in particular that passage we have chosen as the center of our analyses, is part of the proclamation of the new ethos: the ethos of the Gospel. In the teaching of Christ, it is deeply connected with awareness of the "beginning," namely with the mystery of creation in its original simplicity and richness. At the same time, the ethos that Christ proclaims in the Sermon on the Mount is realistically addressed to "historical man," who has become the man of lust. Lust in its three forms, in fact, is the heritage of the whole of mankind, and the human "heart" really participates in it.

Christ, who knows "what is in every man" (cf. Jn. 2:25),[2] cannot speak in any other way than with this awareness. From this point of view, in the words of Matthew 5:27-28 it is not the accusation that prevails but the judgment: a realistic judgment on the human heart, a judgment which, on the one hand, has an anthropological foundation, and, on the other hand, a directly ethical character. For the ethos of the Gospel it is a constitutive judgment.

3. In the Sermon on the Mount, Christ addresses directly the man who belongs to a well-defined society. The Master, too, belongs to that society, to that people. So we must look in Christ's words for a reference to the facts, the situations, the institutions, with which He was familiar in everyday life. These references must be analyzed at least in a summary way, in order that the ethical meaning of the words of Matthew 5:27-28 may emerge more clearly.

However, with these words, Christ also addresses, in an indirect but real way, every "historical" man (understanding this adjective mainly in a theological sense). And this man is precisely the "man of lust," whose mystery and whose heart is known to Christ ("for he himself knew what was in man" Jn. 2:25). The words of the Sermon on the Mount enable us to establish a contact with the interior experience of this man almost at every geographical latitude and longitude, in the various ages, in the different social and cultural conditionings. The man of our time feels called by name with this statement of Christ, no less than the man of "that time," whom the Master was addressing directly.

4. The universality of the Gospel, which is not at all a generalization, lies in this. And perhaps precisely in this statement of Christ,

which we are analyzing here, this is manifested
with particular clarity. By virtue of this statement, the man of all times and all places feels
called, in an adequate, concrete, unrepeatable
way: precisely because Christ appeals to the
human "heart," which cannot be subject to
any generalization. With the category of the
"heart," everyone is characterized individually,
even more than by name, is reached in what
determines him in a unique and unrepeatable
way, is defined in his humanity "from within."

5. The image of the man of lust concerns
his inner being in the first place.[3] The history of
the human "heart" after original sin is written
under the pressure of lust in its three forms,
with which even the deepest image of ethos in
its various historical documents is also connected. However, that inner being is also the
force that decides "exterior" human behavior,
and also the form of multiple structures and
institutions at the level of social life. If we
deduce the content of ethos, in its various
historical formulations, from these structures
and institutions, we always meet this inner
aspect, characteristic of the interior image of
man. This, in fact, is the most essential element. The words of Christ in the Sermon on
the Mount, and especially those of Matthew
5:27-28, indicate it unmistakably. No study on
human ethos can regard it with indifference.

Therefore, in our subsequent reflections,
we shall try to analyze in a more detailed way
that statement of Christ which says: "You have

heard that it was said, 'You shall not commit adultery.' But I say to you that everyone who looks at a woman lustfully has already committed adultery with her in his heart" (or "has already made her adulterous in his heart").

To understand this text better, we shall first analyze its single parts, so as to obtain afterwards a deeper overall view. We shall take into consideration not only those for whom it was intended at that time—those who actually heard the Sermon on the Mount—but also, as far as possible, modern men, the men of our time.

FOOTNOTES

1. The Greek term sklerokardía was formed by the authors of the Septuagint to express what in the Hebrew meant: "non-circumcision of the heart" (cf. e.g.: Dt. 10:16; Jer. 4:4; Sir. 3:26f.) and which, in the literal translation of the New Testament, appears only once (Acts 7:51).

"Non-circumcision" meant "paganism," "immodesty," "distance from the covenant with God"; "non-circumcision of the heart" expressed unyielding obstinacy in opposing God. This is confirmed by the exclamation of the deacon Stephen: "You stiff-necked people, uncircumcised in heart and ears, you always resist the Holy Spirit. As your fathers did, so do you" (Acts 7:51).

So "hardness of heart" must be understood in this philological context.

2. Cf. Rv. 2:23: "...he who searches mind and heart..."; Acts 1:24: "Lord, who knows the hearts of all men..." (kardiognostes).

3. "For out of the heart come evil thoughts, murder, adultery, fornication, theft, false witness, slander. These are what defile a man..." (Mt. 15:19-20).

Content of Commandment: You Shall Not Commit Adultery

General audience of August 13, 1980.

1. Christ's affirmation made during the Sermon on the Mount regarding adultery and "desire," which He calls "adultery of the heart," must be analyzed from the very beginning. Christ says: "You have understood that it was said: You shall not commit adultery..." (Mt. 5:27). He has in mind God's commandment, the sixth in the Decalogue, included in the so-called second Table of the Law which Moses received from God-Yahweh.

First of all, let's place ourselves in the situation of the audience present during the Sermon on the Mount, those who actually heard the words of Christ. They are sons and daughters of the chosen people—people who had received the "law" from God-Yahweh Himself. These people had also received the "prophets" who, time and time again throughout the centuries, had reproved the people's behavior regarding this very commandment, and the way in which it was continually broken. Christ also speaks of similar transgressions. But He speaks more precisely about a certain human interpretation of the law, which negates and does away with the correct meaning of right and wrong as specified by the will of the divine Legislator. The law is, in fact, above all, a means—an indispensable means if "justice is to abound" (Mt. 5:20). Christ desires such justice to be "superior to that of the scribes and Pharisees." He does not accept the interpretation which through the centuries they gave to the authentic content of the law, inasmuch as such content, or rather the purpose and will of the Legislator, were subjected in a certain way to the varied weaknesses and limits of human will power deriving precisely from the threefold concupiscence. This was a casuistic interpretation which was superimposed on the original version of right and wrong connected with the law of the Decalogue. If Christ tends to transform the ethos, He does so mainly to recover the fundamental clarity of the interpretation: "Do not think that I have come to abolish the law or the prophets; I have not come to abolish but to fulfill" (Mt. 5:17). Fulfillment is conditioned by a correct understanding, and this is applied, among others, also to the commandment: "You shall not commit adultery."

IN OLD TESTAMENT TIMES

2. Those who follow the history of the chosen people from the time of Abraham in the pages of the Old Testament will find many facts

which bear witness as to how this commandment was put into practice, and as a result of
such practice, how the casuistic interpretation
of the law developed. First of all, it is well
known that the history of the Old Testament is
the scene for the systematic defection from
monogamy, which fact must have a fundamental significance in our understanding of the prohibition: "You shall not commit adultery."
Especially at the time of the patriarchs, the
abandonment of monogamy was dictated by
the desire for offspring, a very numerous offspring. This desire was so profound, and procreation as the essential end of marriage was so
evident, that wives who loved their husbands
but were not able to give them children, on their
own initiative asked their husbands who loved
them, if they could carry "on their own knees,"
or welcome, his children born of another
woman, for example, those of the serving
woman, the slave. Such was the case of Sarah
regarding Abraham[1] or the case of Rachel and
Jacob.[2] These two narratives reflect the moral
atmosphere in which the Decalogue was practiced. They illustrate the way in which the
Israelite ethos was prepared to receive the commandment, "You shall not commit adultery,"
and how such a commandment was applied in
the most ancient tradition of this people. The
authority of the patriarchs was, in fact, the
highest in Israel and had a religious character.
It was strictly bound to the covenant and to the
promise.

AWARENESS OF DAVID

3. The commandment, "You shall not commit adultery," did not change this tradition. Everything points to the fact that its further development was not limited by the motives (however exceptional) which had guided the behavior of Abraham and Sarah, or of Jacob and Rachel. If we take as an example the most renowned Israelites after Moses, the kings of Israel, David and Solomon, the description of their lives shows the establishing of real polygamy, which was undoubtedly for reasons of concupiscence.

In the history of David, who also had other wives, we are struck not only by the fact that he had taken the wife of one of his subjects, but also by the fact that he was clearly aware of having committed adultery. This fact, as well as the repentance of the king, is described in a detailed and evocative way.[3] Adultery is understood as meaning only the possession of another man's wife, but it is not considered to be the possession of other women as wives together with the first one. All Old Testament tradition indicates that the real need for monogamy as an essential and indispensable implication of the commandment, "You shall not commit adultery," never reached the conscience and the ethos of the following generations of the chosen people.

WITHIN SPECIAL LIMITS

4. Against this background one must also understand all the efforts which aim at putting

the specific content of the commandment, "You shall not commit adultery," within the framework of the promulgated laws. It is confirmed by the books of the Bible in which we find the Old Testament legislation fully recorded as a whole. If we take into consideration the letter of such legislation, we find that it takes a determined and open stand against adultery, using radical means, including the death penalty.[4] It does so, however, by effectively supporting polygamy, even fully legalizing it, at least indirectly. Therefore, adultery was opposed only within special limits and within the sphere of definitive premises which make up the essential form of the Old Testament ethos. Adultery is understood above all (and maybe exclusively) as the violation of man's right of possession regarding each woman who may be his own legal wife (usually, one among many). On the contrary, adultery is not understood as it appears from the point of view of monogamy as established by the Creator. We know now that Christ referred to the "beginning" precisely in regard to this argument (Mt. 19:8).

VOICE OF CONSCIENCE

5. Furthermore, the occasion in which Christ takes the side of the woman caught in adultery and defends her from being stoned to death is most significant. He says to the accusers: "Whoever of you is without sin, let him throw the first stone" (Jn. 8:7). When they put down the stones and go away He says to the

woman: "Go, and from now on, sin no more" (Jn. 8:11). Therefore, Christ clearly identifies adultery with sin. On the other hand, when He turns to those who wanted to stone the adulteress, He does not refer to the precepts of Israel's law but exclusively to conscience. The discernment between right and wrong engraved on the human conscience can show itself to be deeper and more correct than the content of a norm.

As we have seen, the history of God's people in the Old Testament (which we have tried to illustrate through only a few examples) takes place mainly outside the normative content contained in God's commandment, "You shall not commit adultery." It went along, so to speak, side by side with it. Christ wants to straighten out these errors, and thus we have His words spoken during the Sermon on the Mount.

FOOTNOTES

1. Cf. Gn. 16:2.
2. Cf. Gn. 30:3.
3. Cf. 2 Sm. 11:2-27.
4. Cf. Lv. 20:10; Dt. 22:22.

Adultery According to the Law and As Spoken by the Prophets

General audience of August 20, 1980.

1. In the Sermon on the Mount, when Christ says: "You have heard that it was said: You shall not commit adultery" (Mt. 5:27), He refers to what each person present knew perfectly well, and by which everyone felt himself bound by virtue of the commandment of God-Yahweh. However, the history of the Old Testament shows us that both the life of the people bound to God-Yahweh by a special covenant, and the life of each single man, often wanders away from this commandment. A brief look at the legislation, of which there is a comprehensive documentation in the books of the Old Testament, also shows this.

The precepts of the law of the Old Testament were very severe. They were also very detailed and entered into the smallest details of the daily life of the people.[1] One can presume that the more the legalizing of actual polygamy became evident in this law, even more the necessity increased to uphold its juridical dimension, and protect its legal limits. Hence, we find the great number of precepts, and also the severity of the punishments provided for by the legislator for the violation of such norms. On the basis of the analysis which we have previously carried out regarding Christ's reference to the "beginning," in His discourse on the indissolubility of marriage and on the "act of repudiation," it is evident that He clearly sees the basic contradiction that the matrimonial law of the Old Testament had hidden within itself by accepting actual polygamy, namely the institution of the concubine, together with legal wives, or else the right of cohabitation with the slave.[2] It can be said that such a right, while it combatted sin, at the same time contained within itself, or rather protected, the "social dimension of sin," which it actually legalized. In these circumstances it became necessary for the fundamental ethical sense of the commandment, "you shall not commit adultery," to also undergo a basic reassessment. In the Sermon on the Mount, Christ reveals that sense again, namely by going beyond its traditional and legal restrictions.

OLD TESTAMENT'S MATRIMONIAL LAW

2. Maybe it is worth adding that in the interpretation of the Old Testament, to the extent that the prohibition of adultery is balanced—you could say—by the compromise with bodily concupiscence, the more the position regarding sexual deviations is clearly determined. This is confirmed by the relevant precepts which provide for the death penalty for

homosexuality and bestiality. Regarding onanism, it had already been condemned in the tradition of the patriarchs (cf. Gn. 38:8-10). The
behavior of Onan, son of Judah (from where we
have the origin of the word "onanism") "...was
displeasing in the sight of the Lord, and he slew
him also" (Gn. 38:10).

The matrimonial law of the Old Testament,
in its widest and fullest meaning, puts in the
foreground the procreative end of marriage and
in certain cases tries to be juridically equitable
in the treatment of the woman and the man—
for example, it says explicitly, regarding the
punishment for adultery: "If a man commits
adultery with his neighbor's wife, both the
adulterer and the adulteress shall be put to
death" (Lv. 20:10)—but on the whole, it judges
the woman with greater severity.

JUDGMENT MARKED
BY AN OBJECTIVISM

3. Maybe the terminology of this legislation should be emphasized. As always in such
cases, the terminology tends to make objective
the sexuality of that time. And this terminology
is important for the completeness of reflections
on the theology of the body. We find the specific
confirmation of the characteristic of shame
which surrounds what pertains to sex in man.
And more than that, what is sexual is in a certain way considered as "impure," especially
when it regards physiological manifestations of

human sexuality. The "discovery of nudity" (Lv. 20:11; 17:21) is branded as being the equivalent of an illicit and completed sexual act; the expression itself seems already eloquent enough here. There is no doubt that the legislator has tried to make use of the terminology relating to the conscience and customs of contemporary society. Therefore, the terminology of the legislation of the Old Testament confirms our conviction that, not only are the physiology of sex and the bodily manifestations of sexual life known to the legislator, but also that these things are evaluated in a specific way. It is difficult to avoid the impression that such an evaluation was of a negative character. Certainly this in no way nullifies the truths which we know from the Book of Genesis, nor does it lay the blame on the Old Testament—and, among others, also on the Books of Laws—as forerunners of a type of Manichaeism. The judgment expressed therein, regarding the body and sex, is not so much "negative" or severe, but rather marked by an objectivism, motivated by a desire to put in order this area of human life. This is not concerned directly with putting some order in the "heart" of man, but with putting order in the entire social life, at the base of which stands, as always, marriage and the family.

PRACTICAL PRECEPTS

4. If we take into consideration the "sexual" problem as a whole, perhaps we should

briefly turn our attention again to another aspect, and that is to the existing bond between morality, law, and medicine, emphasized in their respective books of the Old Testament. These contain many practical precepts regarding hygiene, or medicine, drawn rather from experience than from science, according to the level reached at that time.[3] And besides, the link between experience and science is distinctly still valid today. In this vast sphere of problems, medicine is always very closely accompanied by ethics; and ethics, as does theology, seeks ways of collaborating with it.

PROPHETS PRESENT ANALOGY

5. In the Sermon on the Mount when Christ spoke the words: "You have heard that it was said: You shall not commit adultery," and He immediately added: "But I say to you...." it is clear that He wanted to restore in the conscience of His audience the ethical significance of this very commandment, disassociating Himself from the interpretation of the "doctors of the law," official experts in it. But other than the interpretation derived from tradition, the Old Testament offers us still another tradition to understand the commandment "do not commit adultery." And it is the tradition of the prophets. In reference to adultery, they wanted to remind "Israel and Judah" that their greatest sin was in abandoning the one true God in favor of the cult of various idols, which the chosen people, in contact with other peoples,

had easily and thoughtlessly adopted. Therefore, a precise characteristic of the language of the prophets is the analogy with adultery, rather than adultery itself; and such analogy also helps to understand the commandment, "do not commit adultery," and the relevant interpretation, the absence of which is noted in the legislative documents. In the pronouncements of the prophets, and particularly of Isaiah, Hosea, and Ezekiel, the God of the Covenant—Yahweh—is often represented as a spouse, and the love which united Him to Israel can and must be identified with the nuptial love of a married couple. And so Israel, because of its idolatry and abandonment of God-the-Spouse, commits, in regard to Him, a betrayal which can be compared to that of a woman in regard to her husband: Israel commits, precisely, "adultery."

LOVE AND BETRAYAL

6. The prophets, using eloquent words, and often by means of images and extraordinarily flexible metaphors, show both the love of Yahweh-Spouse and the betrayal of Israel-Spouse who gives itself over to adultery. This is a theme which must be taken up again in our meditations, that is, when we will analyze the question of the "sacrament"; however, we must already touch on the subject, inasmuch as it is necessary to understand the words of Christ, according to Matthew 5:27-28, to appreciate that renewal of the ethos, implied in these words: "But I say unto you...." If on the one

hand, Isaiah[4] in his texts lays emphasis, above all, on the love of Yahweh-Spouse who always takes the first step towards His spouse, passing over all her infidelities, on the other hand, Hosea and Ezekiel abound in comparisons, which clarify primarily the ugliness and moral evil of the adultery by Israel-the-Spouse.

In the next meditation we will try to penetrate still more profoundly the texts of the prophets, to further clarify the content which, in the conscience of those present during the Sermon on the Mount, corresponded to the "commandment": "you shall not commit adultery."

FOOTNOTES

1. Cf., for example, Dt. 21:10-13; Nm. 30:7-16; Dt. 24:1-4; Dt. 22:13-21; Lv. 20:10-21 and others.

2. Although the Book of Genesis may present the monogamous marriages of Adam, of Seth and Noah, as models to be imitated, and seems to condemn bigamy which only appears among Cain's descendants, (cf. Gn. 4:19), nevertheless, the lives of the patriarchs provide other examples to the contrary. Abraham observes the precepts of the law of Hammurabi, which allowed the taking of a second wife in marriage if the first wife was sterile, and Jacob had two wives and two concubines (cf. Gn. 30:1-19).

The Book of Deuteronomy admits the legal existence of bigamy (cf. Dt. 21:15-17) and even of polygamy, warning the king not to have too many wives (cf. Dt. 17:17); it also confirms the institution of concubines—prisoners of war (cf. Dt. 21:10-14) or even slaves (cf. Est. 21:7-11). (Cf. R. De Vaux, *Ancient Israel, Its Life and Institutions,* London 1976, Darton, Longman, Todd; pp. 24-25, 83). In the Old Testament there is no explicit mention of the obligation of monogamy, although the picture given in the following books shows that it prevailed in the social practice (cf., for example, the Books of Wisdom, except Sirach 37:11; Tobit).

3. Cf., for example, Lv. 12:1-6; 15:1-28; Dt. 21:12-13.

4. Cf., for example, Is. 54; 62:1-5.

Adultery: A Breakdown
of the Personal Covenant

General audience of August 27, 1980.

1. In the Sermon on the Mount Christ says: "Think not that I have come to abolish the Law and the Prophets; I have come not to abolish them but to fulfill them" (Mt. 5:17). In order to understand clearly what such a fulfillment consists of, He then passes on to each single commandment, referring also to the one which says: "You shall not commit adultery." Our previous meditation aimed at showing in what way the correct content of this commandment, desired by God, was obscured by the numerous compromises in the particular legislation of Israel. The prophets, who in their teachings often denounce the abandonment of the true God-Yahweh by the people, comparing it to "adultery," point out such content in a very true way.

Hosea, not only with words, but (as it seems) also in his behavior, is anxious to reveal to us,[1] that the people's betrayal is similar to that in marriage, or rather, even more, to adultery practiced as prostitution: "Go, take to yourself a wife of harlotry, and have children of harlotry, for the land commits great harlotry by

forsaking the Lord" (Hos. 1:2). The prophet
takes heed within himself of this command and
accepts it as coming from God-Yahweh: "and
the Lord said to me, 'Go again, love a woman
who is beloved of a paramour and is an adulteress' " (Hos. 3:1). In fact, although Israel may
be so unfaithful with regard to its God, like the
wife who "went after her lovers and forgot me"
(Hos. 2:13), nevertheless Yahweh never ceases
to search for His spouse, and does not tire of
waiting for her conversion and her return con-
firming this attitude with the words and actions
of the prophet: "And in that day, says the Lord,
you will call me, 'My Husband,' and no longer
will you call me, 'My Ba'al'.... And I will betroth
you to me forever; I will betroth you to me in
righteousness and in justice, in steadfast love
and mercy. I will betroth you to me in faithfulness; and you shall know the Lord" (Hos.
2:16, 19-20). This fervent call to conversion of
the unfaithful wife-consort goes hand in hand
with the following threat: "That she put away
harlotry from her face, and her adultery from
between her breasts; lest I strip her naked and
make her as in the day she was born" (Hos.
2:4-5).

2. The unfaithful Israel-spouse was reminded of this image of the humiliating nudity
of birth, by the prophet Ezekiel, and even within a wider sphere[2] "...but you were cast out
on the open field, for you were abhorred, on the
day that you were born. And when I passed by
you, and saw you weltering in your blood, I said

to you in your blood, 'Live, and grow up like a plant in the field.' And you grew up and became tall and arrived at full maidenhood; your breasts were formed, and your hair had grown; yet you were naked and bare. When I passed by you again and looked upon you, behold, you were at the age for love; and I spread my skirt over you, and covered your nakedness: yea, I plighted my troth to you and entered into a covenant with you, says the Lord God, and you became mine.... And I put a ring on your nose, and earrings in your ears, and a beautiful crown upon your head. Thus you were decked with gold and silver; and your raiment was of fine linen, and silk and embroidered cloth.... And your renown went forth among the nations because of your beauty, for it was perfect through the splendor which I had bestowed upon you.... But you trusted in your beauty, and played the harlot because of your renown, and lavished your harlotries on any passer-by.... How lovesick is your heart, says the Lord God, seeing you did all these things, the deeds of a brazen harlot, making your lofty place in every square. Yet you were not like a harlot, because you scorned hire. Adulterous wife, who receives strangers instead of her husband!'' (Ez. 16:5-8, 12-15, 30-32)

3. The quotation is a little long; however, the text is so important that it was necessary to bring it up again. The analogy between adultery and idolatry is expressed therein in a particularly strong and exhaustive

way. The similarity between the two parts of the analogy consists in the covenant accompanied by love. Out of love, God-Yahweh settles the covenant with Israel—which is not worthy of it—and for Him Israel becomes as a most affectionate, attentive, and generous spouse-consort is towards his own wife. Yahweh-Spouse receives in exchange for this love, which ever since the dawning of history accompanies the chosen people, numerous betrayals: "haughtiness"—here we have the cult of idols, in which "adultery" is committed by Israel-spouse. In the analysis we are carrying out here, the essential thing is the concept of adultery, as put forth by Ezekiel. However, it can be said that the situation as a whole, in which this concept is included (in the analogical sphere), is not typical. Here it is not so much a question of the mutual choice made by the husband and wife, which is born from mutual love, but of the choice of the wife (which was already made at the moment of her birth), a choice deriving from the love of the husband, a love which on the part of the husband himself, is an act of pure mercy. This choice is outlined in the following way: it corresponds to that part of the analogy which defines the covenant of Yahweh with Israel; but on the other hand, it corresponds to a lesser degree to the second part of it, which defines the nature of marriage. Certainly, the mentality of that time was not very sensitive to this reality—according to the Israelites, marriage was rather the result of a unilateral choice, often made by the parents—nevertheless, such a situation seldom forms part of our mentality.

4. Apart from this detail, we must be aware that in the texts of the prophets can be noted a different meaning of adultery from that given by the legislative tradition. Adultery is a sin because it constitutes the breakdown of the personal covenant between the man and the woman. In the legislative texts, the violation of the right of ownership is pointed out, and primarily the right of ownership of the man in regard to that woman who was his legal wife: one of many. In the text of the prophets, the background of real and legalized polygamy does not alter the ethical meaning of adultery. In many texts monogamy appears as the only correct analogy of monotheism as understood in the categories of the covenant, that is, of faithfulness and confidence towards the one true God-Yahweh: Spouse of Israel. Adultery is the antithesis of that nuptial relationship. It is the antinomy of marriage (even as an institution) inasmuch as the monogamous marriage accomplishes within itself the interpersonal alliance of the man and the woman, and achieves the alliance born from love and received by both parties, precisely as marriage (and, as such, is recognized by society). This type of covenant between two people constitutes the foundation of that union when "man...cleaves to his wife and they become one flesh" (Gn. 2:24). In the above-mentioned con-

text, one can say that such bodily union is their "right" (bilateral), but above all that it is the regular sign of the communion of the two people, a union formed between the man and the woman in the capacity of husband and wife. Adultery committed by either one of them is not only the violation of this right, which is exclusive to the other marriage partner, but at the same time it is a radical falsification of this sign. It seems that in the pronouncements of the prophets, precisely this aspect of adultery is expressed in a sufficiently clear manner.

5. In observing that adultery is a falsification of that sign which has not so much its "legality," but rather its simple interior truth in marriage—that is, in the cohabitation of the man and the woman who have become a married couple—then, in a certain sense, we refer again to the basic statements made previously, considering them essential and important for the theology of the body, from both an ethical and anthropological point of view. Adultery is "a sin of the body." All the tradition of the Old Testament bears witness to it, and Christ confirms it. The comparative analysis of His words, pronounced in the Sermon on the Mount (Mt. 5:27-28), like the several relevant enunciations contained in the Gospels and in other parts of the New Testament, allows us to establish the exact reason for the "sinfulness" of adultery. And it is obvious that we determine such reason for "sinfulness," or rather for moral evil, basing ourselves on the principle of contraposition, in

regard to that moral goodness which is faithfulness in marriage, that goodness which can be adequately achieved only in the exclusive relationship of both the parties (that is, in the marriage relationship between a man and a woman). Such a relationship needs precisely nuptial love, the interpersonal structure of which (as we have already pointed out) is governed by the interior "normativity" of the "communion of the two people concerned." It is precisely this which gives a fundamental significance to the covenant (either in the relationship of man-woman, or, analogously, in the relationship of Yahweh-Israel). One can pronounce judgment on the basis of the contraposition of the marriage pact as it is understood, with adultery, its sinfulness, and the moral evil contained in it.

6. All this must be kept in mind when we say that adultery is a "sin of the body"; the "body" is considered here in the conceptual bond with the words of Genesis 2:24, which, in fact, speaks of the man and the woman, who, as husband and wife, unite so closely as to form "one body only." Adultery indicates an act through which a man and a woman, who are not husband and wife, unite as "one body only" (that is, those who are not husband and wife in a monogamous sense, as was originally established, rather than in the legal casuistic sense of the Old Testament). The "sin" of the body can be identified only in regard to the relationship between the people concerned. One can speak

of moral good and evil according to whether in
this relationship there is a true "union of the
body" and whether or not it has the character of
the truthful sign. In this case, we can therefore
judge adultery as a sin, according to the objective content of the act.

This is the content which Christ has in
mind when, in the Sermon on the Mount, He
reminds us: "You have understood that it was
said: You shall not commit adultery." However
Christ does not dwell on such an aspect of the
problem.

FOOTNOTES

1. Cf. Hos. 1-3.
2. Cf. Ez. 16:5-8, 12-15, 30-32.

Meaning of Adultery Transferred from the Body to the Heart

General audience of September 3, 1980.

1. In the Sermon on the Mount Christ limited Himself to recalling the commandment: "You shall not commit adultery," without evaluating the relative behavior of His listeners. What we previously said concerning this theme comes from other sources, especially from Christ's discussion with the Pharisees, in which He hearkened back to the "beginning" (cf. Mt. 19:8; Mk. 10:6). In the Sermon on the Mount Christ omitted such evaluation, or rather, He implied it. What He will say in the second part of the statement, which begins with the words: "But I say to you...," will be something more than the dispute with the "doctors of the law" or with the moralists of the Torah. And it will also be something more with respect to the evaluation of the Old Testament ethos. It will be a direct transition to the new ethos. Christ seems to leave aside the whole dispute about the ethical significance of adultery on the plane

of legislation and casuistry—in which the essential interpersonal relationship between husband and wife was considerably darkened by the objective relationship of property—and it acquires another dimension. Christ says: "But I say to you that everyone who looks at a woman lustfully has already committed adultery with her in his heart" (Mt. 5:28; when reading this passage there always comes to mind the ancient translation: "he has already made her an adulteress in his heart," a version that perhaps better than the present text expresses the fact that here it deals with a purely interior and unilateral act). Thus, therefore, "adultery committed in the heart" is in a certain sense counterposed with "adultery committed in the body." We should question ourselves on the reason why the point of gravity of sin is shifted, and further ask ourselves what is the authentic significance of the analogy. If in fact "adultery," according to its fundamental meaning, can be only a "sin committed in the body," in what sense does what man commits in his heart deserve to be also called adultery? The words with which Christ poses the foundation of the new ethos demand for their part a thorough grounding in anthropology. Before satisfying these queries, let us pause for a while on the expression that, according to Matthew 5:27-28, in a certain way effects the transfer or rather the shifting of the significance of adultery of the "body" to the "heart." These are words which concern desire.

REQUIRES SPECIAL ANALYSIS

2. Christ speaks of concupiscence: "Whoever looks lustfully." This expression requires a special analysis in order to understand the statement in its entirety. It is necessary here to go back to the preceding analysis that aims, I would say, at reconstructing the image of "the lustful man" dating back to the beginning of history (cf. Gn. 3). The man Christ is speaking about in the Sermon on the Mount—the man who "looks lustfully"—is without doubt the concupiscent man. For this very reason, because it is part of bodily concupiscence, he "desires" and "looks lustfully." The figure of the concupiscent man, reconstructed in the preceding aspect, will aid us now in interpreting "desire" about which Christ speaks according to Matthew 5:27-28. This concerns here not only a psychological interpretation, but at the same time a theological interpretation. Christ speaks in the context of human experience and simultaneously in the context of the work of salvation. These two contexts in a certain way are superimposed upon and pervade one another; and that has an essential and elemental significance for the entire ethos of the Gospel, and in particular for the content of the word "lust" or "looking lustfully."

RELEVANT IN EVERY TIME AND PLACE

3. Using such expressions, the Master first refers to the experience of those who are His

direct listeners, then He also refers to the experience and conscience of the man of every time and place. In fact, although evangelical language may have a universal communicativeness, yet for a direct listener, whose conscience was formed on the Bible, "lust" must be linked with numerous precepts and warnings, present in the first place in the Wisdom Books, which contain repeated admonitions about concupiscence of the body and also advice as to how to preserve oneself from it.

4. As we know, Wisdom tradition had an especial interest for the ethics and morality of the Israelite society. What strikes us immediately in these admonitions and advice, appearing for example in the Book of Proverbs[1] and Sirach[2] or even Ecclesiastes,[3] is a certain one-sidedness they have in that the admonitions are above all directed to men. This can mean that for them they are particularly necessary. As far as woman is concerned, it is true that in these warnings and advices she appears most frequently as an occasion of sin or as a downright seducer of whom to beware. Yet one must recognize that both the Book of Proverbs and the Book of Sirach, besides the warning to beware of woman and the seduction of her charm which lead man to sin (cf. Prv. 5:1-6; 6:24-29; Sir. 26:9-12), also praise woman who is the "perfect life companion of her own husband" (cf. Prv. 31:10ff.), and likewise praise the beauty and graciousness of a good wife who is able to make her husband happy.

"A modest wife adds charm to charm, / and no balance can weigh the value of a chaste soul. / Like the sun rising in the heights of the Lord, / so is the beauty of a good wife in her well-ordered home. / Like the shining lamp on the holy lampstand, / so is a beautiful face on a stately figure. / Like pillars of gold on a base of silver, / so are beautiful feet with a steadfast heart.... / A wife's charm delights her husband, / and her skill puts fat on his bones" (Sir. 26:15-18, 13).

WARNING AGAINST TEMPTATION

5. In Wisdom tradition a frequent admonition is in contrast with the above praise of the woman-wife: it is the one that refers to the beauty and graciousness of the woman who is not one's own wife and is the cause of temptation and occasion for adultery: "Do not desire her beauty in your heart..." (Prv. 6:25). In Sirach (cf. 9:8-9) the same warning is expressed in a more peremptory manner: "Turn away your eyes from a shapely woman, / and do not look intently at beauty belonging to another. / Many have been misled by a woman's beauty, / and by it passion is kindled like a fire" (Sir. 9:8-9).

The sense of the Wisdom texts has a prevalent pedagogical significance. They teach virtue and seek to protect the moral order, going back to God's law and to widely under-

stood experience. Moreover, they are distinguished for their special knowledge of the
human "heart." We can say that they develop a
specific moral psychology, yet without falling
into psychologism. In a certain sense, they are
close to that call of Christ to the "heart" that
Matthew has handed down to us (cf. 5:27-28),
even though it cannot be affirmed that they
reveal any tendency to change ethos in a fundamental way. The authors of these books use
the conscience of human inner life to teach
morals somewhat in the sphere of ethos histor-
ically in action, and substantially confirmed
by them. Sometimes one of them, as for example Ecclesiastes, synthesizes this confirmation
with its own "philosophy" of human existence,
which however, if it has an influence on the
method with which warnings and advices are
formulated, does not change the fundamental
structure of ethical evaluation.

"WISDOM" A TRADITION
OF PREPARATION

6. For such transformation it is necessary
to wait until the Sermon on the Mount.
Nonetheless, this very sagacious knowledge of
human psychology present in Wisdom tradition was certainly not without significance for
the circle of personal and immediate hearers of
this sermon. If by virtue of the prophetic tradition these listeners were in a certain sense
prepared for understanding in an adequate way

the concept of "adultery," likewise by virtue of Wisdom tradition they were prepared to understand the words that referred to the "lustful look" or alternatively to "adultery committed in the heart."

It will be well for us to come back again to analysis of concupiscence in the Sermon on the Mount.

FOOTNOTES

1. Cf., e.g., Prv. 5:3-6, 15-20; 6:24—7:27; 21:9, 19; 22:14; 30:20.
2. Cf., e.g., Sir. 7:19, 24-26; 9:1-9; 23:22-27; 25:13-26, 18; 36:21-25; 42:6, 9-14.
3. Cf., e.g., Eccl. 7:26-28; 9:9.

Concupiscence as a Separation from Matrimonial Significance of the Body

General audience of September 10, 1980.

1. Let us reflect on the following words of Jesus, taken from the Sermon on the Mount: "Everyone who looks at a woman lustfully has already committed adultery with her in his heart" ("has already made her an adulteress in his heart") (Mt. 5:28). Christ said this sentence before listeners who, on the basis of the books of the Old Testament, were in a certain sense prepared to understand the significance of the look that comes from concupiscence. Last Wednesday we made reference to the texts taken from the so-called Wisdom Books.

Here is, for example, another passage in which the biblical author analyzes the state of the soul of the man dominated by concupiscence of the flesh: "...the soul heated like a burning fire / will not be quenched until it is consumed; / a man who commits fornication... / will never cease until the fire burns him up; / to a fornicator all bread tastes sweet, / he will never cease until he dies. / A man who breaks his marriage vows / says to himself: 'Who sees me? / Darkness surrounds me, and the walls hide me; / no one sees me. Why should I fear? /

The Most High will not take notice of my sins.' /
His fear is confined to the eyes of men; / he does
not realize that the eyes of the Lord / are ten
thousand times brighter than the sun; / they
look upon all the ways of men, / and perceive
even the hidden places. / So it is with a woman
who leaves her husband, / and provides an heir
by a stranger" (Sir. 23:17-22).

2. Analogous descriptions are not lacking
in world literature.[1] Certainly, many of them
are distinguished by a more penetrating discernment of psychological analysis and a more
intense significance and expressive force. Yet,
the biblical description from Sirach (23:17-22)
includes some elements maintained to be "classic" in the analysis of carnal concupiscence.
One element of this kind, for example, is comparison between concupiscence of the flesh
and fire: this, flaring up in man, invades his
senses, excites his body, involves his feelings
and in a certain sense takes possession of his
"heart." Such passion, originating in carnal
concupiscence, suffocates in his "heart" the
most profound voice of conscience, the sense
of responsibility before God; and in fact that
is particularly placed in evidence in the biblical text just now quoted. On the other hand,
external modesty with respect to men does
persist...or rather an appearance of decency,
which shows itself as fear of the consequences
rather than of the evil in itself. In suffocating
the voice of conscience, passion carries with
itself a restlessness of the body and the senses:

it is the restlessness of the "external man." When the internal man has been reduced to silence, then passion, once it has been given freedom of action, so to speak, exhibits itself as an insistent tendency to satisfy the senses and the body.

This gratification, according to the criterion of the man dominated by passion, should put out the fire; but on the contrary, it does not reach the source of internal peace and only touches the outermost level of the human individual. And here the biblical author rightly observes that man, whose will is committed to satisfying the senses, finds neither peace nor himself, but, on the contrary, "is consumed." Passion aims at satisfaction; therefore it blunts reflective activity and pays no attention to the voice of conscience; thus, without itself having any principle of indestructibility, it "wears out." The dynamism of usage is natural for its continuity, but it tends to exhaust itself. It is true that where passion enters into the whole of the most profound energies of the spirit, it can also become a creative force, in which case, however, it must undergo a radical transformation. If instead it suppresses the deepest forces of the heart and conscience (as occurs in the text of Sirach 23:17-22), it "wears out" and indirectly, man, who is its prey, is consumed.

3. When Christ in the Sermon on the Mount speaks of the man who "lusts," who "looks lustfully," it can be presumed that He had before His eyes also the images known to His lis-

teners from the Wisdom tradition. Yet, at the same time He refers to every man who on the basis of his own internal experience knows the meaning of "lust," "looking at lustfully." The Master does not analyze this experience nor does He describe it, as had for example Sirach (23:17-22); He seems to presuppose, I would say, an adequate knowledge of that interior fact, to which He calls the attention of His listeners, present and potential. Is it possible that some of them do not know what it is all about? If they really know nothing about it, the content of Christ's words would not apply to them, nor would any analysis or description be capable of explaining it to them. If instead they know—this in fact in such case deals with a knowledge completely internal, intrinsic to the heart and the conscience—they will immediately understand when the quoted words refer to them.

4. Christ, therefore, does not describe or analyze what constitutes the experience of "lust," the experience of concupiscence of the flesh. One has even the impression that He does not penetrate this experience in all the breadth of its interior dynamism, as occurs, for example, in the text quoted from Sirach, but rather He pauses on its threshold. "Lust" has not yet been changed into an exterior action, it has still not become the "act of the body"; it is till now the interior act of the heart: it expresses itself in a look, in the way of "looking at the woman." Nevertheless, it already lets itself be under-

stood, it reveals its content and its essential quality. It is now necessary for us to make this analysis. A look expresses what is in the heart. A look expresses, I would say, the man within. If in general it is maintained that man "acts according to his lights" *(operari sequitur esse),* Christ in this case wants to bring out that the man "looks" in conformity with what he is: *intueri sequitur esse.* In a certain sense, man by his look reveals himself to the outside and to others; above all he reveals what he perceives on the "inside."[2]

5. Christ, then, teaches us to consider a look almost like the threshold of inner truth. In a look, "in the way in which one looks," it is already possible to single out completely what is concupiscence. Let us try to explain it. "Lust," "looking at lustfully," indicates an experience of value to the body, in which its "nuptial" significance ceases to be that, just because of concupiscence. Its procreative meaning likewise ceases (we spoke about this in our previous considerations); and when it concerns the conjugal union of man and woman, it is rooted in the nuptial meaning of the body and almost organically emerges from it. Now then, man, "lusting," "looking at lustfully" (as we read in Mt. 5:27-28) attempts in a more or less explicit way the separation of that meaning of the body, that (as we have already observed in our reflections) is at the basis of the communion of persons: whether outside of marriage, or—in a special way—when man and woman are called

to build their union "in the body" (as the "gospel of the beginning" proclaims in the classic text of Gn. 2:24). The experience of the nuptial meaning of the body is subordinate in a special way to the sacramental call, but is not limited to this. Such meaning qualifies the liberty of the gift that—as we shall see more precisely in further analyses—can be fulfilled not only in marriage but also in a different way.

Christ says: "Everyone who looks at a woman lustfully has already committed adultery with her in his heart" ("has made her an adulteress in his heart") (Mt. 5:28). Did He not perhaps mean by this that concupiscence itself —like adultery—is an interior separation from the nuptial meaning of the body? Did He not want to refer His listeners to their internal experiences of such detachment? Is it not perhaps for this reason that He defines it "adultery committed in the heart"?

FOOTNOTES

1. Cf. *Confessions of St. Augustine:* VI, 12, 21, 22; VII, 17; VIII, 11. Dante, *The Divine Comedy,* "Inferno" V, 37-43. C. S. Lewis, *The Four Loves,* New York 1960, Harcourt, Brace, p. 28.

2. A philological analysis confirms the significance of the expression *ho blépon* ("one who looks"; Mt. 5:28).

"If *blépo* of Mt. 5:28 has the value of internal perception, equivalent to 'I think, I pay attention to, I look'—a more precise and more sublime evangelical teaching may result regarding the interpersonal relationship among the disciples of Christ.

"According to Jesus not just a lustful glance makes a person adulterous, but a thought in the heart suffices" (M. Adinolfi, "The desire of a woman in Matthew 5:28" in *Fondamenti biblici della teologia morale.* Proceedings of 22nd Italian Biblical Week, Brescia 1973, Paideia, p. 279).

Mutual Attraction
Differs from Lust

General audience of September 17, 1980.

1. During our last reflection, we asked ourselves what was the "lust" of which Christ spoke in the Sermon on the Mount (Mt. 5:27-28). Let us recall that He spoke of it in relation to the commandment: "Do not commit adultery." "Lust" itself (more exactly: "looking at lustfully") is defined as "adultery committed in the heart." That gives much food for thought. In the preceding reflections we said that Christ, by expressing Himself in that way, wanted to indicate to His listeners the separation from the matrimonial significance of the body felt by a human being (in this case the man) when concupiscence of the flesh is coupled with the inner act of "lust." The separation of the matrimonial significance of the body causes at the same time a conflict with his personal dignity: a veritable conflict of conscience.

At this point it appears that the biblical meaning (hence also theological) of "lust" is different from the purely psychological. The latter describes "lust" as an intense inclination towards the object because of its particular value: in the case considered here, its "sexual" value. As it seems, we will find such definition in most of the works dealing with similar themes. Yet, the biblical interpretation, while not underestimating the psychological aspect, places that ethic in relief above all, since there is a value that is being impaired. "Lust," I would say, is a deception of the human heart in the perennial call of man and woman—a call revealed in the very mystery of creation—to communion by means of mutual giving. So then, when Christ in the Sermon on the Mount (Mt. 5:27-28) makes reference to the "heart" or the internal man, His words do not cease being charged with that truth concerning the "principle" to which, in replying to the Pharisees (cf. Mt. 19:8), He had reverted to the whole problem of man, woman and marriage.

2. The perennial call, which we have tried to analyze following the Book of Genesis (especially Gn. 2:23-25) and, in a certain sense, the perennial mutual attraction on man's part to femininity and on woman's part to masculinity, is an indirect invitation of the body, but it is not lust in the sense of the word of Matthew 5:27-28. "Lust" that carries into effect the concupiscence of the flesh (also and especially in the purely internal act) diminishes the significance of what were—and that in reality do not cease being—that invitation and that reciprocal attraction. The "eternal feminine" *(das ewig weibliche),* just like the "eternal masculine," for that matter, on the level of historicity, too, tends to free itself from pure concupiscence and seeks a position of achieve-

ment in the world of people. It testifies to that original sense of shame of which Genesis 3 speaks. The dimension of intentionality of thought and heart constitutes one of the main streams of universal human culture. Christ's words in the Sermon on the Mount exactly confirm this dimension.

3. Nonetheless, these words clearly assert that "lust" is a real part of the human heart. When we state that "lust," when compared with the original mutual attraction of masculinity and femininity, represents a "reduction," we have in mind an intentional "reduction," almost a restriction or closing down of the horizon of mind and heart. In fact, it is one thing to be conscious that the value of sex is a part of all the rich storehouse of values with which the female appears to the man; it is another to "reduce" all the personal riches of femininity to that single value, that is, of sex, as a suitable object for the gratification of sexuality itself. The same reasoning can be valid concerning what masculinity is for the woman, even though Matthew's words in 5:27-28 refer directly to the other relationship only. The intentional "reduction" is, as can be seen, primarily of an axiological nature. On one hand the eternal attraction of man towards femininity (cf. Gn. 2:23) frees in him—or perhaps it should free—a gamut of spiritual-corporal desires of an especially personal and "sharing" nature (cf. analysis of the "beginning"), to which a proportionate pyramid of values corresponds. On the

other hand, "lust" limits this gamut, obscuring the pyramid of values that marks the perennial attraction of male and female.

4. "Lust" has the internal effect, that is, in the "heart," on the interior horizon of man and woman, of obscuring the significance of the body, of the person itself. Femininity thus ceases being above all else an object for the man; it ceases being a specific language of the spirit; it loses its character of being a sign. It ceases, I would say, bearing in itself the wonderful matrimonial significance of the body. It ceases its correlation to this significance in the context of conscience and experience. "Lust" arising from concupiscence of the flesh itself, from the first moment of its existence within the man—its existence in his "heart"—passes in a certain sense close to such a context (one could say, using an image, that it passes on the ruins of the matrimonial significance of the body and all its subjective parts) and by virtue of axiological intentionality itself aims directly at an exclusive end: to satisfy only the sexual need of the body, as its precise object.

5. Such an intentional and axiological reduction can take place, according to the words of Christ (Mt. 5:27-28), in the sphere of the "look" (of "looking") or rather in the sphere of a purely interior act expressed by the look. A look (or rather "looking") is in itself a cognitive act. When concupiscence enters into its inner structure, the look takes on the character of "lustful knowledge." The biblical expression "to look at

lustfully'' can indicate both a cognitive act, which the lusting man "makes use of," (that is, giving him the character of lust aiming at an object), and a cognitive act that arouses lust in the other object and above all in its will and in its "heart." As is seen, it is possible to place an intentional interpretation on an interior act, being aware of one and the other pole of man's psychology: knowledge or lust understood as *appetitus* (which is something broader than "lust," since it indicates everything manifested in the object as "aspiration," and as such always tends to aim at something, that is, towards an object known under the aspect of value). Yet, an adequate interpretation of the words of Matthew 5:27-28 requires us—by means of the intentionality itself of knowledge or of the "appetitus" to discern something more, that is, the intentionality of the very existence of man in relation to the other man: in our case, of the man in relation to the woman and the woman in relation to the man.

It will be well for us to return to this subject. Concluding today's reflection, it is necessary to add again that in that "lust," in "looking at lustfully," with which the Sermon on the Mount deals, the woman, for the man who "looks" in that way, ceases to exist as an object of eternal attraction and begins to be only an object of carnal concupiscence. To that is connected the profound inner separation of the matrimonial significance of the body about which we already spoke in the preceding reflection.

Depersonalizing Effect of Concupiscence

General audience of September 24, 1980.

1. In the Sermon on the Mount Christ says: "You have heard that it was said, You shall not commit adultery. But I say to you that everyone who looks at a woman lustfully has already committed adultery with her in his heart" (Mt. 5:27-28). We have been trying for some time to penetrate the meaning of this statement, analyzing the single elements in order better to understand the text as a whole.

When Christ speaks of a man who "looks lustfully," He indicates not only the dimension of intentionality in "looking," and so lustful knowledge, the psychological dimension, but also the dimension of the intentionality of man's very existence. In the situation described by Christ, that dimension passes unilaterally from the man, who is the subject, to the woman, who has become the object (this does not mean, however, that such a dimension is only unilateral). For the present we will not reverse the situation analyzed, or extend it to both parties, to both subjects. Let us dwell on the situation outlined by Christ, stressing that it is a question of a "purely interior" act, hidden in the heart and stopping on the threshold of the look.

It is enough to note that in this case the woman, who—owing to her personal subjectivity exists perennially "for man," waiting for him, too, for the same reason, to exist "for her"—is deprived of the meaning of her attraction as a person, who, though being characteristic of the "eternal feminine," becomes at the same time only an object for the man: she begins, that is, to exist intentionally as an object for the potential satisfaction of the sexual need inherent in his masculinity. Although the act is completely interior, hidden in the "heart" and expressed only by the "look," there already occurs in him a change (subjectively unilateral) of the very intentionality of existence. If it were not so, if it were not a question of such a deep change, the following words of the same sentence: "has already committed adultery with her in his heart" (Mt. 5:28), would have no meaning.

2. That change of the intentionality of existence, by means of which a certain woman begins to exist for a certain man not as a subject of call and personal attraction or as a subject "of communion," but exclusively as an object for the potential satisfaction of the sexual need, is carried out in the "heart" since it is carried out in the will. Cognitive intentionality itself does not yet mean enslavement of the "heart." Only when the intentional reduction, illustrated previously, sweeps the will along into its narrow horizon, when it brings forth the decision of a relationship with another human being (in our case: with the woman) according to the

specific scale of values of "lust," only then can it be said that "desire" has also gained possession of the "heart." Only when "lust" has gained possession of the will is it possible to say that it is dominant over the subjectivity of the person and that it is at the basis of the will, and the possibility of choosing and deciding, through which—by virtue of self-decision or self-determination—the very way of existing with regard to another person is established. The intentionality of this existence then acquires a full subjective dimension.

3. Only then—that is from that subjective moment and on its subjective prolongation—is it possible to confirm what we read, for example, in Sirach (23:17-22) about the man dominated by lust, and what we read in even more eloquent descriptions in world literature. Then we can also speak of that more or less complete "compulsion," which is called elsewhere "compulsion of the body" and which brings with it loss of the "freedom of the gift," congenital in deep awareness of the matrimonial meaning of the body, of which we have also spoken in preceding analyses.

4. When we speak of "desire" as the transformation of the intentionality of a concrete existence, of the man, for example, for whom (according to Mt. 5:27-28) a certain woman becomes merely the object of the potential satisfaction of the "sexual need" inherent in his masculinity, it is not at all a matter of ques-

tioning that need, as an objective dimension of human nature with the procreative finality that is characteristic of it. Christ's words in the Sermon on the Mount (in its whole broad context) are far from Manichaeism, as the true Christian tradition also is. In this case, there cannot arise, therefore, objections of the kind. It is a question, on the contrary, of the man's and the woman's way of existing as persons, that is, of that existing in a mutual "for," which—also on the basis of what, according to the objective dimension of human nature, can be defined as the "sexual need"—can and must serve the building up of unity "of communion" in their mutual relations. Such, in fact, is the fundamental meaning characteristic of the perennial and reciprocal attraction of masculinity and femininity, contained in the very reality of the constitution of man as a person, body and sex together.

5. The possible circumstance that one of the two persons exists only as the subject of the satisfaction of the sexual need, and the other becomes exclusively the object of this satisfaction, does not correspond to the union or personal "communion," to which man and woman were mutually called "from the beginning"—on the contrary it is in conflict with it. Moreover, the case in which both the man and the woman exist reciprocally as the object of satisfaction of the sexual need, and each on his or her part is only the subject of that satisfaction, does not correspond to this unity of "communion"—but

on the contrary clashes with it. This "reduction" of such a rich content of the reciprocal and perennial attraction of human persons in their masculinity or femininity, does not at all correspond to the "nature" of the attraction in question. This "reduction," in fact, extinguishes the personal meaning, "of communion," characteristic of man and woman, through which, according to Genesis 2:24, "a man...cleaves to his wife, and they become one flesh." "Lust" turns away the intentional dimension of the man's and woman's mutual existence from the personal perspectives, "of communion," characteristic of their perennial and mutual attraction, reducing it, and, so to speak, pushing it towards utilitarian dimensions, within which the human being "uses" the other human being, for the sake merely of satisfying his own "needs."

6. It seems possible to find this content again, charged with human interior experience characteristic of different ages and environments, in Christ's concise affirmation in the Sermon on the Mount. At the same time, we cannot in any case lose sight of the meaning that this affirmation attributes to man's "interiority," to the integral dimension of the "heart" as the dimension of the inner man. Here lies the very core of the transformation of ethos aimed at by Christ's words according to Matthew 5:27-28, expressed with powerful forcefulness and at the same time with admirable simplicity.

Establishing the Ethical Sense

General audience of October 1, 1980.

1. We arrive in our analysis at the third part of Christ's enunciation in the Sermon on the Mount (Mt. 5:27-28). The first part was: "You have heard that it was said, You shall not commit adultery." The second: "But I say to you that everyone who looks at a woman lustfully," is grammatically connected with the third part: "has already committed adultery with her in his heart."

The method applied here, which is that of dividing, of "splitting" Christ's enunciation into three parts which follow one another, may seem artificial. However, when we seek the ethical meaning of the whole enunciation in its totality, the division of the text used by us may, precisely, be useful, provided that it is applied not only in a disjunctive, but in a conjunctive way. And that is what we intend to do. Each of the distinct parts has its own specific content and connotations, and this is precisely what we wish to stress by dividing the text. But it must be pointed out at the same time that each of the parts is explained in direct relationship with the others. That refers in the first place to the principal semantic elements, by which the enunciation constitutes a whole. Here are these elements: to commit adultery, to desire to commit adultery in the body, to commit adultery in the heart. It would be particularly difficult to establish the ethical sense of "desiring" without the element indicated here last, that is "adul-tery in the heart." The preceding analysis has already taken this element into consideration to a certain extent; however, a fuller understand-ing of the part: "to commit adultery in the heart" is possible only after a special analysis.

REDISCOVERING VALUES

2. As we have already mentioned at the beginning, it is a question here of establishing the ethical sense. Christ's enunciation in Mat-thew 5:27-28 starts from the commandment: "Do not commit adultery," in order to show how it must be understood and put into prac-tice, so that the "justice" that God-Yahweh wished as Legislator may abound in it: in order that it may abound to a greater extent than appeared from the interpretation and casuistry of the Old Testament doctors. If Christ's words in this sense aim at constructing the new ethos (and on the basis of the same commandment), the way to that passes through the rediscovery of the values which—in general Old Testament understanding and in the application of this commandment—have been lost.

THAT JUSTICE MAY ABOUND

3. From this point of view also the formu-lation of the text of Matthew 5:27-28 is sig-

nificant. The commandment "do not commit
adultery" is formulated as a prohibition which
categorically excludes a given moral evil. It is
well known that the same law (the ten commandments), as well as the prohibition "do not
commit adultery," also includes the prohibition
"do not covet your neighbor's wife" (Ex. 20:14,
17; Dt. 5:18, 21). Christ does not nullify one prohibition with regard to the other. Although He
speaks of "desire," He aims at a deeper clarification of "adultery." It is significant that after
mentioning the prohibition "do not commit
adultery," as well known to His listeners, subsequently, in the course of His enunciation He
changes His style and the logical structure from
the normative to the narrative-affirmative.
When He says: "Everyone who looks at a
woman lustfully has already committed adultery with her in his heart," He describes an
interior fact, whose reality can easily be
understood by His listeners. At the same time,
through the fact thus described and qualified,
He indicates how the commandment: "Do not
commit adultery" must be understood and put
into practice, so that it will lead to the "justice"
willed by the Legislator.

ESTABLISHING THE SENSE

4. In this way we have reached the expression "has committed adultery in his heart," the
key-expression, as it seems, for understanding
its correct ethical meaning. This expression is
at the same time the principal source for reveal-

ing the essential values of the new ethos: the ethos of the Sermon on the Mount. As often happens in the Gospel, here, too, we come up against a certain paradox. How, in fact, can "adultery" take place without "committing adultery," that is, without the exterior act which makes it possible to identify the act forbidden by the law? We have seen how much the casuistry of the "doctors of the law" devoted itself to defining this very problem. But even apart from casuistry, it seems clear that adultery can be identified only "in the flesh," that is, when the two, the man and the woman who unite with each other in such a way as to become one flesh (cf. Gn. 2:24), are not legal spouses, husband and wife. What meaning, then, can "adultery committed in the heart" have? Is it not, perhaps, just a metaphorical expression used by the Master to highlight the sinfulness of lust?

ETHICAL CONSEQUENCES

5. If we admitted this semantic reading of Christ's enunciation (Mt. 5:27-28), it would be necessary to reflect deeply on the ethical consequences that would be derived from it, that is, on the conclusions about the ethical regularity of the behavior. Adultery takes place when the man and the woman who unite with each other so as to become one flesh (cf. Gn. 2:24), that is, in the way characteristic of spouses, are not legal spouses. The detecting of adultery as a sin committed "in the body" is closely and exclusively united with the "exterior" act, with living

together in a conjugal way, which refers also to the status of the acting persons, recognized by society. In the case in question, this status is improper and does not authorize such an act (hence, precisely, the term "adultery").

THE AFFIRMATIVE ANSWER

6. Going on to the second part of Christ's enunciation (that is, the one in which the new ethos begins to take shape) it would be necessary to understand the expression: "Everyone who looks at a woman lustfully," in exclusive reference to persons according to their civil status, that is, their status recognized by society, whether or not they are husband and wife. Here the questions begin to multiply. Since there can be no doubt about the fact that Christ indicates the sinfulness of the interior act of lust expressed through a way of looking at every woman who is not the wife of the one who so looks at her, therefore we can and even must ask ourselves if, with the same expression, Christ admits and approves such a look, such an interior act of lust, directed towards the woman who is the wife of the man who so looks at her.

The following logical premise seems to be in favor of the affirmative answer to such a question: (in the case in question) only the man who is the potential subject of "adultery in the flesh" can commit "adultery in the heart." Since this subject cannot be the man-husband with regard to his own legitimate wife, therefore "adultery in the heart" cannot refer to him, but any other man can be considered guilty of it. If he is the husband, he cannot commit it with regard to his own wife. He alone has the exclusive right to "desire," to "look lustfully" at the woman who is his wife—and never can it be said that due to such an interior act he deserves to be accused of "adultery committed in the heart." If by virtue of marriage he has the right to "unite with his wife," so that "the two become one flesh," this act can never be called "adultery." Similarly the interior act of "desire," dealt with in the Sermon on the Mount, cannot be defined "adultery committed in the heart."

CONSIDERING THE RESULTS

7. This interpretation of Christ's words in Mt. 5:27-28 seems to correspond to the logic of the ten commandments, in which, in addition to the commandment "do not commit adultery" (VI), there is also the commandment "do not covet your neighbor's wife" (IX). Furthermore, the reasoning that has been made in support of it has all the characteristics of objective correctness and accuracy. Nevertheless, there remain good grounds for doubt whether this reasoning takes into account all the aspects of revelation, as well as of the theology of the body, which must be considered, especially when we wish to understand Christ's words. We have already seen previously what is the "specific

weight" of this expression, how rich are the anthropological and theological implications of the one sentence in which Christ refers "to the beginning" (cf. Mt. 19:8). The anthropological and theological implications of the enunciation in the Sermon on the Mount in which Christ refers to the human heart confer on the enunciation itself also a "specific weight" of its own, and at the same time determine its consistency with evangelical teaching as a whole. And therefore we must admit that the interpretation presented above, with all its objective correctness and logical precision, requires a certain amplification and, above all, a deepening. We must remember that the reference to the human heart, expressed perhaps in a paradoxical way (Mt. 5:27-28), comes from Him who "knew what was in man" (Jn. 2:25). And if His words confirm the Decalogue (not only the sixth, but also the ninth), at the same time they express that knowledge of man, which—as we have pointed out elsewhere—enables us to unite awareness of human sinfulness with the perspective of the "redemption of the body" (cf. Rom. 8:23). This very knowledge lies at the basis of the new ethos which emerges from the words of the Sermon on the Mount.

Taking all that into consideration, we conclude that, as in understanding "adultery in the flesh" Christ criticizes the erroneous and one-sided interpretation of adultery that is derived from the failure to observe monogamy (that is marriage understood as the indefectible covenant of persons), so also in understanding "adultery in the heart" Christ not only takes into consideration the real juridical status of the man and woman in question, but also makes the moral evaluation of the "desire" depend above all on the personal dignity itself of the man and the woman. And this has its importance both when it is a question of persons who are not married, and—perhaps even more— when they are spouses, wife and husband. From this point of view it will be useful for us to complete the analysis of the words of the Sermon on the Mount.

Interpreting the Concept of Concupiscence

General audience of October 8, 1980.

1. Today I wish to conclude the analysis of the words spoken by Christ in the Sermon on the Mount on "adultery" and "lust," and in particular of the last element of this enunciation, in which "lust of the eyes" is defined specifically as "adultery committed in the heart."

We have already previously seen that the above-mentioned words are usually understood as desire for another's wife (that is, according to the spirit of the ninth commandment of the Decalogue). It seems, however, that this interpretation—a more restrictive one—can and must be widened in the light of the total context. The moral evaluation of lust (of "looking lustfully"), which Christ calls "adultery committed in the heart," seems to depend above all on the personal dignity itself of man and of woman. This holds true both for those who are not united in marriage, and—perhaps even more—for those who are husband and wife.

NEED TO AMPLIFY

2. The analysis which we have made so far of the enunciation of Matthew 5:27-28: "You have heard that it was said, You shall not commit adultery. But I say to you that everyone who looks at a woman lustfully has already committed adultery with her in his heart," indicates the necessity of amplifying and above all deepening the interpretation presented previously, with regard to the ethical meaning that this enunciation contains. Let us dwell on the situation described by the Master, a situation in which the one who "commits adultery in his heart" by means of an interior act of lust (expressed by the look) is the man. It is significant that Christ, speaking of the object of this act, does not stress that it is "another man's wife," or a woman who is not his own wife, but says generically: a woman. Adultery committed "in the heart" is not circumscribed in the limits of the interpersonal relationship which make it possible to determine adultery committed "in the body." It is not these limits that decide exclusively and essentially about adultery committed "in the heart," but the very nature of lust, expressed in this case by a look, that is, by the fact that that man—of whom Christ speaks, for the sake of example—"looks lustfully." Adultery "in the heart" is committed not only *because* man "looks" in this way at a woman who is not his wife, but *precisely* because he looks at a woman in this way. Even if he looked

in this way at the woman who is his wife, he could likewise commit adultery "in his heart."

TO SATISFY HIS OWN INSTINCT

3. This interpretation seems to take into consideration more amply what has been said about lust in these analyses as a whole, and primarily about the lust of the flesh as a permanent element of man's sinfulness (status naturae lapsae). The lust which, as an interior act, springs from this basis (as we tried to indicate in the preceding analyses) changes the very intentionality of the woman's existence "for" man, reducing the riches of the perennial call to the communion of persons, the riches of the deep attractiveness of masculinity and femininity, to mere satisfaction of the sexual "need" of the body (with which the concept of "instinct" seems to be linked more closely). As a result of this reduction, the person (in this case, the woman) becomes for the other person (the man) mainly the object of the potential satisfaction of his own sexual "need." In this way, that mutual "for" is distorted, losing its character of communion of persons in favor of the utilitarian function. A man who "looks" in this way, as Matthew 5:27-28 writes, "uses" the woman, her femininity, to satisfy his own "instinct." Although he does not do so with an exterior act, he has already assumed this attitude deep down, inwardly deciding in this way with regard to a given woman. This is what adultery "committed in the heart" consists of.

Man can commit this adultery "in the heart" also with regard to his own wife, if he treats her only as an object to satisfy instinct.

BETTER INTERPRETATION

4. It is not possible to arrive at the second interpretation of the words of Matthew 5:27-28, if we confine ourselves to the purely psychological interpretation of lust without taking into account what constitutes its specific theological character, that is, the organic relationship between lust (as an act) and the lust of the flesh, as, so to speak, a permanent disposition derived from man's sinfulness. The purely psychological (or "sexological") interpretation of "lust" does not seem to constitute a sufficient basis to understand the text of the Sermon on the Mount in question. If, on the other hand, we refer to the theological interpretation—without underestimating what remains unchangeable in the first interpretation (the psychological one)—it, that is, the second interpretation (the theological one), appears to us as more complete. Thanks to it, in fact, also the ethical meaning of the key-enunciation of the Sermon on the Mount, to which we owe the adequate dimension of the ethos of the Gospel, becomes clearer.

FULFILLMENT IN THE HEART

5. Sketching this dimension, Christ remains faithful to the law. "Think not that I have come to abolish the law and the prophets;

I have come not to abolish them but to fulfill them" (Mt. 5:17). Consequently He shows
how deep down it is necessary to go, how
the recesses of the human heart must be
thoroughly revealed, in order that this heart
may become a place of "fulfillment" of the law.
The enunciation of Matthew 5:27-28, which
makes manifest the interior perspective of
adultery committed "in the heart"—and in this
perspective points out the right ways to fulfill
the commandment: "do not commit adultery"
—is an extraordinary argument. This enunciation (Mt. 5:27-28) refers, in fact, to the sphere
in which it is a question in particular of "purity
of heart" (cf. Mt. 5:8) (an expression which—as
is known—has a wide meaning in the Bible).
Elsewhere, too, we will have the opportunity to
consider in what way the commandment "do
not commit adultery"—which, as regards the
way in which it is expressed and the content,
is a univocal and severe prohibition (like the
commandment: "You shall not covet your
neighbor's wife," Ex. 20:17)—is carried out
precisely by means of "purity of heart." The
severity and strength of the prohibition are
testified to directly by the following words of the
text of the Sermon on the Mount, in which
Christ speaks figuratively of "plucking out
one's eye" and "cutting off one's hand," if these
members were the cause of sin (cf. Mt. 5:29-30).
We have seen previously that the legislation of
the Old Testament, though abounding in severe
punishments, did not contribute to "fulfill the
law," because its casuistry was marked by

many compromises with the lust of the flesh. Christ teaches, on the contrary, that the commandment is carried out through "purity of heart," which is not given to man unless at the cost of firmness with regard to everything that springs from the lust of the flesh. He who is able to demand consistently from his "heart" and from his "body," acquires "purity of heart."

TWO BECOME ONE FLESH

6. The commandment "do not commit adultery" finds its rightful motivation in the indissolubility of marriage, in which man and woman, by virtue of the original plan of the Creator, unite in such a way that "the two become one flesh" (cf. Gn. 2:24). Adultery, by its essence, is in conflict with this unity, in the sense in which this unity corresponds to the dignity of persons. Christ not only confirms this essential ethical meaning of the commandment, but aims at strengthening it in the very depth of the human person. The new dimension of *ethos* is always connected with the revelation of that depth, which is called "heart," and with its liberation from "lust," in order that man, male and female in all the interior truth of the mutual "for," may shine forth more fully in that heart. Freed from the constraint and from the impairment of the spirit that the lust of the flesh brings with it, the human being, male and female, finds himself mutually in the freedom of

the gift which is the condition of all life together in truth, and, in particular, in the freedom of mutual giving, since both, as husband and wife, must form the sacramental unity willed, as Genesis 2:24 says, by the Creator Himself.

MUTUAL RELATIONSHIP

7. As is plain, the necessity which, in the Sermon on the Mount, Christ lays on all His actual and potential listeners, belongs to the interior space in which man—precisely the one who is listening to Him—must perceive anew the lost fullness of his humanity, and want to regain it. That fullness in the mutual relationship of persons, of the man and of the woman, is claimed by the Master in Matthew 5:27-28, having in mind above all the indissolubility of marriage, but also every other form of the common life of men and women, that common life which constitutes the pure and simple fabric of existence. Human life, by its nature, is "coeducative" and its dignity, its balance, depend, at every moment of history and at every point of geographical longitude and latitude, on "who" she will be for him, and he for her.

The words spoken by Christ in the Sermon on the Mount have certainly this universal and at the same time profound significance. Only in this way can they be understood in the mouth of Him who knew thoroughly "what was in man," and who, at the same time, bore within

Him the mystery of the "redemption of the body," as St. Paul will put it. Are we to fear the severity of these words, or rather have confidence in their salvific content, in their power?

In any case, the analysis carried out of the words spoken by Christ in the Sermon on the Mount opens the way to further indispensable reflections in order to reach full awareness of "historical" man, and above all of modern man.

Interpretation
and Misunderstandings

The following article appeared in the daily L'Osservatore Romano *on October 12, 1980. It was in response to widespread reaction to Pope John Paul's message in the general audience of October 8, 1980.*

The word of the Pope has an intrinsic value of its own which is derived from the mandate given by Christ to Peter and his Successors. This value is recognized by believers who accept pontifical teaching as the Magisterium of the Vicar of Christ, while by others, non-believers, it may be accepted with more or less favor and even rejected, since the motives of faith which induce believers to accept it, do not exist. All this responds to normal rules of behavior and free choice before facts that fall under the sphere of faith. What does not fall under this sphere, on the contrary, is superficiality, lack of respect, and absence of attention which leads to wanting to take up a position in any case, without the due objective reading of the word, yielding to misunderstandings, we hope in good faith.

Certainly, the Magisterium of the Pope may not always be easy and simple. Sometimes, owing to the very complexity of the subject, it is expressed in articulated or even difficult forms, difficult of access to listeners lacking an adequate cultural background. That does not mean that the word of the Pope is something reserved for the elite; but that sometimes it requires a cultural or catechetical meditation such that the Magisterium, while preserving the dignity and rigor of form, may become bread broken for all. Nothing of all this happens when someone takes a sentence of the pontifical Magisterium out of context and, heedless of the complexity and the completeness of the discourse, ventures upon interpretations and comments so improvised and absurd as to be stupifying.

On Wednesday, the Pope delivered an address that can really be catalogued among those that call for attention, ability to read, rigor of interpretation, and completeness of examination. The subject of adultery has been prepared for by weeks of catechesis on the theology of marriage and of the body, the meaning of marital love, the interiority of the act of love, and the meaning of lust and of looking. The Wednesday address opens with an enunciation which is then amply explained and analyzed in all its aspects. The sentence that was taken out of its context and is part of the initial enunciation is the following: *Adultery "in the heart" is committed not only because man "looks" in this way at a woman who is not his wife, but precisely because he looks at a woman in this way. Even if he looked in this way at the woman who is his wife, he could likewise commit adultery "in his heart."* This sentence cannot be taken as a pretext to concoct absurd comments which lead to the conclusion that the conjugal relationship has been declared adulterous: this cannot be done especially when what is said afterwards on the dignity of the human person, the meaning of the gift in contrast to possession and appropriation, is ignored, and without quoting in full at least this other sentence: "Man can commit this adultery 'in the heart' also with regard to his own wife, *if he treats her only as an object to satisfy instinct.*"

Unless one has a merely juridical and positivistic idea of ethics, it is not possible, we believe, to reduce the illicit to the illegal, and therefore to limit the concept of adultery to the exterior act as an offense. Since man's moral life is entirely integrated in the completeness of his free personality, it is the fruit of a series of choices that start "from the heart," understood as man's deep orientation, and are manifested in exterior acts. To adulterate a relationship means, even in the metaphorical sense, to distort it, pollute it as compared with its original meaning. Now what is it, if not adultery, to reduce the conjugal relationship to a mere satisfaction of sexual need? A man who "looks with desire," that is, merely lustfully at his own wife, certainly cannot be said to "love" his wife and take up an attitude of donation towards her. In reality he does not love his wife, but himself, and he commits adultery precisely for this reason, because the destination of his own love, which has become selfishness, is different and mistaken.

Has it not been said and written plainly in recent years that marriage often becomes a condition of slavery especially for the woman; that she is reduced to an erotic object or even that in certain cases the conjugal relationship is only masked prostitution: housework and the satisfaction of man's instincts in exchange for maintenance and the matrimonial "status" for the woman? These are things said and written by sources that certainly cannot be suspected of excessive obedience to the Church, and sustained, in particular, by those movements of opinion which intend, often rightly, to defend woman's dignity. They are things which, to a great extent, start from analysis of situations that actually exist.

Now it is impossible to see how anyone can fail to grasp in the Pope's words a passionate defense of the dignity of the relationship between man and woman in marriage, precisely when he says that the original nature of this relationship, when expressed in "reifying" (depersonalizing) desire, is polluted, so that it becomes similar to an adultery.

The suspicion arises then that not all the mistaken interpretations are in good faith. Perhaps precisely on the part of certain environments sick of male chauvinism, a defensive life, so to speak, is being prepared in defense of "privileges" and abuses against the woman-wife; abuses and privileges which people are trying so laboriously to demolish? Obviously what is said of the man with regard to the woman also holds true vice versa.   CLAUDIO SORGI

Gospel Values
and Duties of the Human Heart

General audience of October 15, 1980.

1. During our many Wednesday meetings, we have made a detailed analysis of the words of the Sermon on the Mount, in which Christ refers to the human "heart." As we now know, His words are exacting. Christ says: "You have heard that it was said, You shall not commit adultery. But I say to you that everyone who looks at a woman lustfully has already committed adultery with her *in his heart*" (Mt. 5:27-28). This reference to the heart throws light on the dimension of human interiority, the dimension of the inner man, characteristic of ethics, and even more of the theology of the body. Desire, which rises in the sphere of the lust of the flesh, is at the same time an interior and theological reality, which is experienced, in a way, by every "historical" man. And it is precisely this man—even if he does not know the words of Christ—who continually asks himself the question about his own "heart." Christ's words make this question particularly explicit: Is the heart accused, or is it called to good? And we now intend to take this question into consideration, towards the end of our

reflections and analyses, connected with the sentence of the Gospel, so concise and yet categorical at the same time, so pregnant with theological, anthropological, and ethical content.

A second question goes hand in hand with it, a more "practical" one: how "can" and "must" he act, the man who accepts Christ's words in the Sermon on the Mount, the man who accepts the *ethos* of the Gospel, and, in particular, accepts it in this field?

ETHOS OF HUMAN PRACTICE

2. This man finds in the considerations made up to now the answer, at least an indirect one, to the two questions: How "can" he act, that is, on what can he rely in his "inner self," at the source of his "interior" or "exterior" acts? And furthermore: How "should" he act, that is, in what way do the values known according to the "scale" revealed in the Sermon on the Mount constitute a duty of his will and his "heart," of his desires and his choices? In what way are they "binding" on him in action, in behavior, if, accepted by means of knowledge, they already "commit" him in thinking and, in a certain way, in "feeling"? These questions are significant for human "praxis," and indicate an organic connection of "praxis" itself with *ethos*. Lived morality is always the *ethos* of human practice.

MORAL SENSITIVITY

3. It is possible to answer the aforesaid questions in various ways. In fact, various answers are given, both in the past and today. That is confirmed by an ample literature. In addition to the answers we find in it, it is necessary to take into consideration the infinite number of answers that concrete man gives to these questions by himself, the ones that his conscience, his awareness and moral sensitivity give repeatedly, in the life of everyone. Precisely in this sphere an *interpenetration of ethos and praxis is carried out.* Here there live their own life (not exclusively "theoretical") the individual principles, that is, the norms of morality with their motivations, worked out and made known by moralists, but also the ones worked out—certainly not without a link with the work of moralists and scientists—by individual men, as authors and direct subjects of real morality, as co-authors of its history, on which there depends also the level of morality itself, its progress or its decadence. In all this there is reconfirmed everywhere, and always, that "historical man" to whom Christ once spoke, proclaiming the good news of the Gospel with the Sermon on the Mount, where He said among other things the sentence that we read in Matthew 5:27-28: "You have heard that it was said, You shall not commit adultery. But I say to you that everyone who looks at a woman lustfully has already committed adultery with her in his heart."

NEED FOR FURTHER ANALYSES

4. Matthew's enunciation is stupendously concise in comparison with everything that has been written on this subject in secular literature. And perhaps its power in the history of *ethos* consists precisely in this. At the same time the fact must be realized that the history of *ethos* flows in a multiform bed, in which the individual currents draw nearer to, or move further away from, one another in turn. "Historical" man always evaluates his own "heart" in his own way, just as he also judges his own "body": and so he passes from the pole of pessimism to the pole of optimism, from puritan severity to modern permissiveness. It is necessary to realize this, in order that the *ethos* of the Sermon on the Mount may always have due transparency with regard to man's actions and behavior. For this purpose it is necessary to make some more analyses.

WORDS MISUNDERSTOOD

5. Our reflections on the meaning of the words of Christ according to Matthew 5:27-28 would not be complete, if they did not dwell—at least briefly—on what can be called the echo of these words in the history of human thought and of the evaluation of *ethos.* The echo is always a transformation of the voice and of the words that the voice expresses. We know from

experience that this transformation is sometimes full of mysterious fascination. In the case in question, it was rather the opposite that happened. Christ's words, in fact, have rather been stripped of their simplicity and depth, and there has been conferred a meaning far removed from the one expressed in them, a meaning that, when all is said and done, is even in contradiction to them. We have in mind here all that happened outside Christianity under the name of Manichaeism,[1] and that also tried to enter the ground of Christianity as regards theology itself and the *ethos* of the body. It is well known that, in its original form, Manichaeism, which arose in the East outside the biblical environment and sprang from Mazdeistic dualism, saw the source of evil in matter, in the body, and therefore proclaimed the condemnation of everything that is corporeal in man. And since corporeity is manifested in man mainly through sex, so the condemnation was extended to marriage and to conjugal life, as well as to other spheres of being and acting in which corporeity is expressed.

AFFIRMATION OF THE BODY

6. To an unaccustomed ear, the evident severity of that system might seem in harmony with the severe words of Matthew 5:29-30, in which Christ speaks of "plucking out one's eye" or "cutting off one's hand," if these members were the cause of scandal. Through the purely "material" interpretation of these ex-

pressions, it was also possible to obtain a Manichaean view of Christ's enunciation, in which He speaks of a man who has "committed adultery in his heart...by looking at a woman lustfully." In this case, too, the Manichaean interpretation aims at condemnation of the body, as the real source of evil, since the "ontological" principle of evil, according to Manichaeism, is concealed and at the same time manifested in it. The attempt was made, therefore, to see *this condemnation in the Gospel, and sometimes it was perceived, where actually only a particular requirement addressed to the human spirit had been expressed.*

Note that the condemnation might—and may always be—a loophole to avoid the requirements set in the Gospel by Him who "knew what was in man" (Jn. 2:25). There is no lack of proofs in history. We have already partially had the opportunity (and we will certainly have it again) to show to what extent such a requirement may arise solely from an affirmation—and not from a denial or a condemnation—if it has to lead to an affirmation that is even more mature and deeper, objectively and subjectively. And the words of Christ according to Matthew 5:27-28 must lead to such an affirmation of the femininity and masculinity of the human being, as the personal dimension of "being a body." This is the right ethical meaning of these words. They impress, on the pages of the Gospel, a peculiar dimension of *ethos* in order to impress it subsequently on human life.

We will try to take up this subject again in our further reflections.

FOOTNOTES

1. Manichaeism contains and brings to maturation the characteristic elements of all "gnosis," that is, the *dualism* of two coeternal and radically opposed principles and the concept of a *salvation* which is realized only through *knowledge* (gnosi) or self-understanding. In the whole Manichaean myth there is only one hero and only one situation which is always repeated: the fallen soul is imprisoned in matter and is liberated by knowledge.

The present historical situation is negative for man, because it is a provisional and abnormal mixture of spirit and matter, good and evil, which presupposes a prior, original state, in which the two substances were separate and independent. There are, therefore, three "Times": "initium," or the original separation; the "medium," that is, the present mixture; and the "finis" which consists in return to the original division, in salvation, implying a complete break between Spirit and Matter.

Matter is, fundamentally, concupiscence, an evil instinct for pleasure, the instinct of death, comparable, if not identical, with sexual desire, "libido." It is a force that tries to attack Light; it is disorderly movement, bestial, brutal, and semiconscious desire.

Adam and Eve were begotten by two demons; our species was born from a series of repelling acts of cannibalism and sexuality and keeps signs of this diabolical origin, which are the body, which is the animal form of the "Archons of hell" and "libido," which drives man to copulate and reproduce himself, that is, to keep his luminous soul always in prison.

If he wants to be saved, man must try to liberate his "living self" *(nous)* from the flesh and from the body. Since Matter has its supreme expression in concupiscence, the capital sin lies in sexual union (fornication), which is brutality and bestiality, and makes men instruments and accomplices of Evil for procreation.

The elect constitute the group of the perfect, whose virtue has an ascetic characteristic, practicing the abstinence
commanded by the three "seals": the "seal of the mouth"
forbids all blasphemy and commands abstention from
meat, blood, wine, all alcoholic drinks; and also fasting; the
"seal of the hands" commands respect of the life (the
"Light") enclosed in bodies, in seeds, in trees, and forbids
the gathering of fruit, the tearing up of plants, the taking of
the life of men and of animals; the "seal of the womb"
prescribes total continence (cf. H. Ch. Puech: *Le Manicheisme; son fondateur—sa doctrine*, Paris, 1949 [Musée
Guimet t. LVI], pp. 73-88; H. Ch. Puech, *Le Manicheisme* in
"Histoire des Religions" [Encyclopedie de la Pleiade] II,
[Gallimard] 1972, pp. 522-645; J. Ties, *Manichéisme*, in
"Catholicisme hier, aujourd'hui, demain, 34, Lille 1977
[Letouzey-Ane pp. 314-320]).

Realization of the Value of the Body According to the Plan of the Creator

General audience of October 22, 1980.

1. At the center of our reflections, at the Wednesday meetings, there has been for a long time now the following enunciation of Christ in the Sermon on the Mount: "You have heard that it was said, You shall not commit adultery. But I say to you that everyone who looks at a woman lustfully has already committed adultery with her (towards her) in his heart" (Mt. 5:27-28). These words have an essential meaning for the whole theology of the body contained in Christ's teaching. Therefore, we rightly attribute great importance to their correct understanding and interpretation. Already in our preceding reflection, we noted that the Manichean doctrine, both in its primitive and in its later expressions, contradicts these words.

It is not possible, in fact, to see in the sentence of the Sermon on the Mount, analyzed here, a "condemnation" or an accusation of the body. If anything, one could catch a glimpse of a condemnation of the human heart. However, the reflections we have made so far show that, if the words of Matthew 5:27-28 contain an accusation, it is directed above all at the man of lust. With those words the heart is not so much accused as subjected to a judgment, or, better, called to a critical, in fact a self-critical, examination: whether or not it succumbs to the lust of the flesh. Penetrating into the deep meaning of the enunciation of Matthew 5:27-28, we must note, however, that the judgment contained in it about "desire," as an act of lust of the flesh, brings with it not the negation, but rather the affirmation, of the body as an element which, together with the spirit, determines man's ontological subjectivity and shares in his dignity as a person. In this way, therefore, the judgment on the lust of the flesh has a meaning essentially different from the one which the Manichaean ontology presupposes and which necessarily springs from it.

BODY MANIFESTS THE SPIRIT

2. The body, in its masculinity and femininity, is called "from the beginning" to become the manifestation of the spirit. It does so also by means of the conjugal union of man and woman, when they unite in such a way as to form "one flesh." Elsewhere (cf. Mt. 19:5-6) Christ defends the inviolable rights of this unity, by means of which the body, in its masculinity and femininity, assumes the value of a sign—in a way, a sacramental sign. Furthermore, by warning against the lust of the flesh, He expresses the same truth about the ontological dimension of the body and confirms its ethical meaning, consistent with His teaching as a whole. This ethical meaning has nothing in

common with the Manichaean condemnation, and is, on the contrary, deeply penetrated by the mystery of the "redemption of the body," of which St. Paul will write in the Letter to the Romans (cf. Rom. 8:23). The "redemption of the body" does not indicate, however, ontological evil as a constituent attribute of the human body, but points out only man's sinfulness, as a result of which he has, among other things, lost the clear sense of the nuptial meaning of the body, in which interior mastery and the freedom of the spirit is expressed. It is a question here—as we have already pointed out previously—of a "partial," potential loss, where the sense of the nuptial meaning of the body is confused, in a way, with lust, and easily lets itself be absorbed by it.

TRANSFORMATION OF CONSCIENCE AND ATTITUDES

3. The appropriate interpretation of Christ's words according to Matthew 5:27-28, as well as the "praxis" in which the authentic ethos of the Sermon on the Mount will be subsequently expressed, must be absolutely free of Manichaean elements in thought and in attitude. A Manichaean attitude would lead to an "annihilation" of the body—if not real, at least intentional—to negation of the value of human sex, of the masculinity and femininity of the human person, or at least to their mere "toleration" in the limits of the "need" delimited by

the necessity of procreation. On the basis of
Christ's words in the Sermon on the Mount, on
the other hand, Christian ethos is characterized
by a transformation of the conscience and attitudes of the human person, both man and
woman, such as to express and realize the value
of the body and of sex, according to the
Creator's original plan, placed as they are in the
service of the "communion of persons," which
is the deepest substratum of human ethics and
culture. Whereas, for the Manichaean mentality, the body and sexuality constitute, so to
speak, an "anti-value"; for Christianity, on the
contrary, they always remain a "value not sufficiently appreciated," as I will explain better further on. The second attitude indicates what
must be the form of ethos in which the mystery
of the "redemption of the body" takes root, so
to speak, in the "historical" soil of man's
sinfulness. That is expressed by the theological
formula, which defines the "state" of "historical" man as *status naturae lapsae simul ac
redemptae.* (The state of fallen, but at the same
time redeemed, nature).

QUESTION OF DETACHMENT

4. Christ's words in the Sermon on the
Mount (Mt. 5:27-28) must be interpreted in the
light of this complex truth about man. If they
contain a certain "accusation" leveled at the
human heart, all the more so they address an
appeal to it. The accusation of the moral evil
which "desire," born of intemperate lust of the

flesh, conceals within itself, is at the same time a call to overcome this evil. And if victory over evil must consist in detachment from it (hence the severe words in the context of Matthew 5:27-28), it is, however, only a question of detaching oneself from the evil of the act (in the case in question, the interior act of "lust"), and never of transferring the negative character of this act to its object. Such a transfer would mean a certain acceptance—perhaps not fully conscious—of the Manichaean "anti-value." It would not constitute a real and deep victory over the evil of the act, which is evil by its moral essence, and so evil of a spiritual nature; on the contrary, there would be concealed in it the great danger of justifying the act to the detriment of the object (the essential error of Manichaean ethos consists, in fact, just in this). It is clear that in Matthew 5:27-28 Christ demands detachment from the evil of "lust" (or of the look of disorderly desire), but His enunciation does not let it be supposed in any way that the object of that desire, that is, the woman who is "looked at lustfully," is an evil. (This clarification seems to be lacking sometimes in some Wisdom texts.)

KNOWING THE DIFFERENCE

5. We must, therefore, specify the difference between the "accusation" and the "appeal." Since the accusation leveled at the evil of lust is at the same time an appeal to overcome it, this victory, consequently, must be united

with an effort to discover the true values of the object, in order that the Manichaean "anti-value" may not take root in man, in his conscience, and in his will. In fact, as a result of the evil of "lust," that is, of the act of which Christ speaks in Matthew 5:27-28, the object to which it is addressed constitutes for the human subject a "value not sufficiently appreciated." If, in the words of the Sermon on the Mount (Mt. 5:27-28) which have been analyzed, the human heart is "accused" of lust (or is warned against that lust), at the same time, by means of the words themselves, it is called to discover the full sense of what, in the act of lust, constitutes for him a "value that is not sufficiently appreciated." As we know, Christ said: "Everyone who looks at a woman lustfully has already committed adultery with her in his heart." "Adultery committed in the heart" can and must be understood as "devaluation," or as the impoverishment of an authentic value, as an intentional deprivation of that dignity to which the complete value of her femininity corresponds in the person in question. The words of Matthew 5:27-28 contain a call to discover this value and this dignity, and to reassert them. It seems that only when the words of Matthew are understood in this way, is their semantic significance respected.

To conclude these concise considerations, it is necessary to note once more that the Manichaean way of understanding and evaluating man's body and sexuality is essentially alien to the Gospel, not in conformity with the exact meaning of the words of the Sermon on the Mount spoken by Christ. The appeal to master the lust of the flesh springs precisely from the affirmation of the personal dignity of the body and of sex, and serves only this dignity. Anyone who wants to see in these words a Manichaean perspective would be committing an essential error.

The Power of Redeeming Completes the Power of Creating

General audience of October 29, 1980.

1. For a long time now, our Wednesday reflections have been centered on the following enunciation of Jesus Christ in the Sermon on the Mount: "You have heard that it was said, You shall not commit adultery. But I say to you that everyone who looks at a woman lustfully has already committed adultery with her (with regard to her) in his heart" (Mt. 5:27-28). We have recently explained that the above-mentioned words cannot be understood or interpreted in a Manichaean way. They do not contain, in any way, a condemnation of the body and of sexuality. They merely contain a call to overcome the three forms of lust, and in particular the lust of the flesh. This call springs

precisely from the affirmation of the personal dignity of the body and of sexuality, and merely confirms this affirmation.

To clarify this formulation, that is, to determine the specific meaning of the words of the Sermon on the Mount, in which Christ appeals to the human heart (cf. Mt. 5:27-28), is important not only because of "inveterate habits," springing from Manichaeanism, in the way of thinking and evaluating things, but also because of some contemporary positions which interpret the meaning of man and of morality. Ricoeur described Freud, Marx and Nietzsche as "masters of suspicion"[1] *("maîtres du soupçon")*, having in mind the set of systems that each of them represents, and above all, perhaps, the hidden basis and the orientation of each of them in understanding and interpreting the *humanum* itself.

It seems necessary to refer, at least briefly, to this basis and to this orientation. It must be done to discover on the one hand a significant convergence, and on the other hand also a fundamental divergence, which has its source in the Bible, to which we are trying to give expression in our analyses. What does the convergence consist of? It consists of the fact that the above-mentioned thinkers, who have exercised, and still do, a great influence on the way of thinking and evaluating of the men of our time, seem substantially also to judge and accuse man's "heart." Even more, they seem to judge it and accuse it because of what, in biblical language, especially Johannine, is called lust, the three forms of lust.

THE PRIDE OF LIFE

2. Here a certain distribution of the parts could be made. In the Nietzschean interpretation, the judgment and accusation of the human heart correspond, in a way, to what is called in biblical language "the pride of life"; in the Marxist interpretation, to what is called "the lust of the eyes"; in the Freudian interpretation, on the other hand, to what is called "the lust of the flesh." The convergence of these conceptions with the interpretation of man founded on the Bible lies in the fact that, discovering the three forms of lust in the human heart, we, too, could have limited ourselves to putting that heart in a state of continual suspicion. However, the Bible does not allow us to stop here. The words of Christ according to Matthew 5:27-28 are such that, while manifesting the whole reality of desire and lust, they do not permit us to make this lust the absolute criterion of anthropology and ethics, that is, the very core of the hermeneutics of man. In the Bible, lust in its three forms does not constitute the fundamental and perhaps even unique and absolute criterion of anthropology and ethics, although it is certainly an important coefficient to understand man, his actions, and their moral value. Also the analysis we have carried out so far shows this.

TO THE "MAN OF LUST"

3. Though wishing to arrive at a complete interpretation of Christ's words on man who "looks lustfully" (cf. Mt. 5:27-28), we cannot be content with any conception of "lust," even if the fullness of the "psychological" truth accessible to us were to be reached; we must, on the contrary, draw upon the First Letter of John 2:15-16 and the "theology of lust" that is contained in it. The man who "looks lustfully" is, in fact, the man of the three forms of lust; he is the man of the lust of the flesh. Therefore he "can" look in this way and he must even be conscious that, leaving this interior act at the mercy of the forces of nature, he cannot avoid the influence of the lust of the flesh. In Matthew 5:27-28 Christ also deals with this and draws attention to it. His words refer not only to the concrete act of "lust," but, indirectly, also to the "man of lust."

ETHOS OF REDEMPTION

4. Why cannot these words of the Sermon on the Mount, in spite of the convergence of what they say about the human heart[2] with what has been expressed in the interpretation of the "masters of suspicion"—why cannot they be considered as the foundation of the aforesaid interpretation or a similar one? And why do they constitute an expression, a configuration, of a completely different ethos?—different not only from the Manichaean one, but also from

the Freudian one? I think that the set of analyses and reflections made so far gives an answer to this question. Summing up, it can be said briefly that Christ's words according to Matthew 5:27-28 do not allow us to stop at the accusation of the human heart and to regard it continually with suspicion, but must be understood and interpreted above all as an appeal to the heart. This derives from the very nature of the ethos of redemption. On the basis of this mystery, which St. Paul (Rom. 8:23) defines "the redemption of the body," on the basis of the reality called "redemption" and, consequently, on the basis of the ethos of the redemption of the body, we cannot stop only at the accusation of the human heart on the basis of desire and lust of the flesh. Man cannot stop at putting the "heart" in a state of continual and irreversible suspicion due to the manifestations of the lust of the flesh and libido, which, among other things, a psychoanalyst perceives by means of analyses of the unconscious.[3] Redemption is a truth, a reality, in the name of which man must feel called, and "called with efficacy." He must realize this call also through Christ's words according to Matthew 5:27-28, reread in the full context of the revelation of the body. Man must feel called to rediscover, nay more, to realize the nuptial meaning of the body and to express in this way the interior freedom of the gift, that is, of that spiritual state and that spiritual power which are derived from mastery of the lust of the flesh.

THAT GOOD BEGINNING

5. Man is called to this by the word of the Gospel, therefore from "outside," but at the same time he is also called from "inside." The words of Christ, who in the Sermon on the Mount appeals to the "heart," induce the listener, in a way, to this interior call. If he lets them act in him, he will be able to hear within him at the same time almost the echo of that "beginning," that good "beginning" to which Christ refers on another occasion, to remind His listeners who man is, who woman is, and who we are for each other in the work of creation. The words of Christ uttered in the Sermon on the Mount are not a call hurled into emptiness. They are not addressed to the man who is completely absorbed in the lust of the flesh, unable to seek another form of mutual relations in the sphere of the perennial attraction, which accompanies the history of man and woman precisely "from the beginning." Christ's words bear witness that the original power (therefore also the grace) of the mystery of creation becomes for each of them power (that is, grace) of the mystery of redemption. That concerns the very "nature," the very substratum of the humanity of the person, the deepest impulses of the "heart." Does not man feel, at the same time as lust, a deep need to preserve the dignity of the mutual relations, which find their expression in the body, thanks to his masculinity and femininity? Does he not feel the need to impregnate them with everything that is noble and

beautiful? Does he not feel the need to confer on them the supreme value which is love?

REAL MEANING OF LIFE

6. Rereading it, this appeal contained in Christ's words in the Sermon on the Mount cannot be an act detached from the context of concrete existence. It always means—though only in the dimension of the act to which it refers —the rediscovery of the meaning of the whole of existence, the meaning of life, in which there is contained also that meaning of the body which here we call "nuptial." The meaning of the body is, in a sense, the antithesis of Freudian libido. The meaning of life is the antithesis of the interpretation "of suspicion." This interpretation is very different, it is radically different from what we rediscover in Christ's words in the Sermon on the Mount. These words reveal not only another ethos, but also another vision of man's possibilities. It is important that he, precisely in his "heart," should not only feel irrevocably accused and given as a prey to the lust of the flesh, but that he should feel forcefully called in this same heart. Called precisely to that supreme value that is love. Called as a person in the truth of his humanity, therefore also in the truth of his masculinity or femininity, in the truth of his body. Called in that truth which has been his heritage "from the beginning," the heritage of his heart, which is deeper than the sinfulness inherited, deeper than lust in its three forms. The words of Christ,

set in the whole reality of creation and redemption, reactivate that deeper heritage and give it real power in man's life.

FOOTNOTES

1. Cf. Paul Ricoeur, *Le conflit des interpretations*, Paris 1969 (Seuil, pp. 149-150).

2. Cf. also Mt. 5:19-20.

3. Cf., for example, the characteristic affirmation of Freud's last work (S. Freud, *Abriss der Psychoanalyse*, *Das Unbehagen der Kultur*, Frankfurt-M. Hamburg 1955 (Fisher), pp. 74-75.

Then that "core" or "heart" of man would be dominated by the union between the erotic instinct and the destructive one, and life would consist in satisfying them.

"Eros" and "Ethos" Meet
and Bear Fruit
in the Human Heart

General audience of November 5, 1980.

1. In the course of our weekly reflections on Christ's enunciation in the Sermon on the Mount, in which, in reference to the commandment, "You shall not commit adultery," He compares "lust" ("looking lustfully") with "adultery committed in the heart," we are trying to answer the question: Do these words only accuse the human "heart," or are they first and foremost an appeal addressed to it? An appeal, of course, of ethical character; an important and essential appeal for the very ethos of the Gospel. We answer that the above-mentioned words are above all an appeal.

At the same time, we are trying to bring our reflections nearer to the "routes" taken, in its sphere, by the conscience of contemporary men. Already in the preceding cycle of our considerations we mentioned "eros." This Greek term, which passed from mythology to philosophy, then to the literary language and finally to the spoken language, unlike the word

"ethos," is alien and unknown to biblical
language. If, in the present analyses of biblical
texts, we use the term "ethos," known to the
Septuagint and to the New Testament, we do so
because of the general meaning it has acquired
in philosophy and theology, embracing in its
content the complex spheres of good and evil,
depending on human will and subject to the
laws of conscience and the sensitivity of the
human "heart." The term "eros," as well as
being the proper name of the mythological
character, has a philosophical meaning in the
writings of Plato,[1] which seems to be different
from the common meaning and also from what
is usually attributed to it in literature. Obviously, we must take into consideration here the
vast range of meanings, which differ from one
another in their finer shades, as regards both
the mythological character and the philosophical content, and above all the "somatic" or
"sexual" point of view. Taking into account
such a vast range of meanings, it is opportune
to evaluate, in an equally differentiated way,
what is related to "eros"[2] and is defined as
"erotic."

CONNOTATION OF
THE TERM "EROS"

2. According to Plato, "eros" represents
the interior force that drags man towards everything good, true, and beautiful. This "attraction" indicates, in this case, the intensity of
a subjective act of the human spirit. In the com-

mon meaning, on the contrary—as also in literature—this "attraction" seems to be first and
foremost of a sensual nature. It arouses the
mutual tendency of both the man and the
woman to draw closer to each other, to the
union of bodies, to that union of which Genesis
2:24 speaks. It is a question here of answering
the question whether "eros" connotes the same
meaning in the biblical narrative (particularly
in Gn. 2:23-25), which certainly bears witness
to the mutual attraction and the perennial call
of the human person—through masculinity and
femininity—to that "unity in the flesh" which,
at the same time, must realize the communion-
union of persons. It is precisely because of this
interpretation of "eros" (as well as of its relationship with ethos) that also the way in which
we understand the "lust" spoken about in the
Sermon on the Mount takes on fundamental
importance.

DANGER OF REDUCTIVISM
AND EXCLUSIVISM

3. As it seems, common language takes into
consideration above all that meaning of "lust,"
which we previously defined as "psychological" and which could also be called "sexological": this is done on the basis of premises
which are limited mainly to the naturalistic,
"somatic" and sensualistic interpretation of
human eroticism. (It is not a question here, in
any way, of reducing the value of scientific

researches in this field, but we wish to call attention to the danger of reductivism and exclusivism.) Well, in the psychological and sexological sense, lust indicates the subjective intensity of straining towards the object because of its sexual character (sexual value). That straining has its subjective intensity due to the specific "attraction" which extends its dominion over man's emotional sphere and involves his "corporeity" (his somatic masculinity or femininity). When in the Sermon on the Mount we hear of the "concupiscence" of the man who "looks at a woman lustfully," these words—understood in the "psychological" (sexological) sense—refer to the sphere of phenomena which in common language are, precisely, described as "erotic." Within the limits of the enunciation of Matthew 5:27-28, it is a question only of the interior act, while it is mainly those ways of acting and of mutual behavior of the man and the woman, which are the external manifestation of these interior acts, that are defined "erotic." Nevertheless, there seems to be no doubt that—reasoning in this way—it is almost necessary to put the sign of equality between "erotic" and what "derives from desire" (and serves to satisfy the lust of the flesh). If this were so, then the words of Christ according to Matthew 5:27-28 would express a negative judgment about what is "erotic" and, addressed to the human heart, would constitute at the same time a severe warning against "eros."

MANY SHADES OF MEANING OF "EROS"

4. However, we have already mentioned that the term "eros" has many semantic shades of meaning. Therefore, wishing to define the relationship of the enunciation of the Sermon on the Mount (Mt. 5:27-28) with the wide sphere of "erotic" phenomena, that is, those mutual actions and ways of behaving through which man and woman approach each other and unite so as to be "one flesh" (cf. Gn. 2:24), it is necessary to take into account the multiplicity of the semantic shades of meaning of "eros." It seems possible, in fact, that in the sphere of the concept of "eros"—taking into account its Platonic meaning—there is room for that ethos, for those ethical and indirectly even theological contents which, in the course of our analyses, have been seen from Christ's appeal to the human "heart" in the Sermon on the Mount. Also knowledge of the multiple semantic nuances of "eros" and of what, in the differentiated experience and description of man, at various periods and various points of geographical and cultural longitude and latitude, is defined as "erotic," can be of help in understanding the specific and complex riches of the "heart," to which Christ appealed in His enunciation in Matthew 5:27-28.

THE "ETHOS" OF REDEMPTION

5. If we admit that "eros" means the interior force that "attracts" man towards what is

true, good, and beautiful, then, within the sphere of this concept, the way towards what Christ wished to express in the Sermon on the Mount, can also be seen to open. The words of Matthew 5:27-28, if they are an "accusation" of the human heart, are at the same time, even more, an appeal made to it. This appeal is the specific category of the ethos of redemption. The call to what is true, good, and beautiful means at the same time, in the ethos of redemption, the necessity of overcoming what is derived from lust in its three forms. It also means the possibility and the necessity of transforming what has been weighed down by the lust of the flesh. Furthermore, if the words of Matthew 5:27-28 represent this call, then they mean that, in the erotic sphere, "eros" and "ethos" do not differ from each other, are not opposed to each other, but are called to meet in the human heart, and, in this meeting, to bear fruit. What is worthy of the human "heart" is that the form of what is "erotic" should be at the same time the form of ethos, that is, of what is "ethical."

ETHOS AND ETHICS

6. This affirmation is very important for ethos and at the same time for ethics. In fact, a "negative" meaning is often connected with the latter concept, because ethics bears with it norms, commandments, and also prohibitions. We are commonly inclined to consider the word of the Sermon on the Mount on "lust" (on "look-

ing lustfully") exclusively as a prohibition—a prohibition in the sphere of "eros" (that is, in the "erotic" sphere). And very often we are content merely with this understanding, without trying to reveal the really deep and essential values that this prohibition covers, that is, ensures. Not only does it protect them, but it also makes them accessible and liberates them, if we learn to open our "heart" to them.

In the Sermon on the Mount Christ teaches us this and directs man's heart toward these values.

FOOTNOTES

1. According to Plato, man, placed between the world of the senses and the world of Ideas, has the destiny of passing from the first to the second. The world of Ideas, however, is not able, by itself, to overcome the world of the senses: only Eros, congenital in man, can do that. When man begins to have a presentiment of Ideas, thanks to contemplation of the objects existing in the world of the senses, he receives the impulse from Eros, that is, from the desire for pure Ideas. Eros, in fact, is the guiding of the "sensual" or "sensitive" man towards what is transcendent: the force that directs the soul towards the world of Ideas. In the "Symposium" Plato describes the stages of this influence of Eros: the latter raises man's soul from the beauty of a single body to that of all bodies, and so to the beauty of knowledge and finally to the very idea of Beauty (cf. *Symposio* 211; *Repubblica* 514).

Eros is neither purely human nor divine: it is something intermediate *(daimonion)* and intermediary. Its principal characteristic is permanent aspiration and desire. Even when it seems to give freely, Eros persists as the "desire of possessing," and yet it is different from purely sensual love, being the love that strives toward the sublime.

According to Plato, the gods do not love because they do not feel desires, since their desires are all satisfied. Therefore, they can only be the object, but not the subject of love

(Symposio 200-201). So they do not have a direct relationship with man; only the mediation of Eros makes it possible for a relationship to be established *(Symposio* 203). Eros is, therefore, the way that leads man to divinity, but not vice-versa.

The aspiration to transcendence is, therefore, a constituent element of the Platonic concept of Eros, a concept that overcomes the radical dualism of the world of Ideas and the world of the senses. Eros makes it possible to pass from one to the other. It is therefore a form of escape beyond the material world, which the soul must renounce, because the beauty of the sensible subject has a value only insofar as it leads higher.

However, Eros always remains, for Plato, egocentric love: it aims at winning and possessing the object which, for man, represents a value. To love good means desiring to possess it forever. Love is, therefore, always a desire for immortality, and that, too, shows the egocentric character of Eros (cf. A. Nygren, *Eros et Agapé. La notion chrétienne de l'amour et ses transformations,* I, Paris, 1962, Aubier, pp. 180-200).

For Plato, Eros is a passing from the most elementary knowledge to deeper knowledge; at the same time it is the aspiration to pass from "that which is not," and is evil, to what "exists in fullness," and is good (cf. M. Scheler, *Amour et connaissance,* in: *"Le sens de la souffrance, suivi de deux autres essais,"* Paris, Aubier, s.d. p. 145).

2. Cf., e.g., C. S. Lewis, "Eros," in *The Four Loves* New York, 1960 (Harcourt, Brace), pp. 131-133, 152, 159-160; P. Chauchard, *Vices des vertus, vertus des vices,* Paris, 1965 (Mame), p. 147.

Spontaneity: The Mature Result of Conscience

General audience of November 12, 1980.

1. Today we resume our analysis, which started a week ago, on the mutual relationship between what is "ethical" and what is "erotic." Our reflections follow the pattern of the words spoken by Christ in the Sermon on the Mount, with which He referred to the commandment "You shall not commit adultery," and, at the same time, defined "lust" ("looking lustfully") as "adultery committed in the heart." We see from these reflections that "ethos" is connected with the discovery of a new order of values. It is necessary continually to rediscover in what is "erotic" the nuptial meaning of the body and the true dignity of the gift. This is the role of the human spirit, a role of an ethical nature. If it does not assume this role, the very attraction of the senses and the passion of the body may stop at mere lust devoid of ethical value, and man, male and female, does not experience that fullness of "eros," which means the aspiration of the human spirit towards what is true, good and beautiful, so that what is "erotic" also becomes true, good and beautiful. It is indispensable, therefore, that ethos should become the constituent form of eros.

FRUIT OF DISCERNMENT

2. The above-mentioned reflections are closely connected with the problem of spontaneity. It is very often thought that it is ethos itself that takes away spontaneity from what is erotic in man's life and behavior; and for this reason detachment from ethos is demanded "for the benefit" of eros. Also the words of the Sermon on the Mount would seem to hinder this "good." But this opinion is erroneous and, in any case, superficial. Obstinately accepting it and upholding it, we will never reach the full dimensions of eros, and that inevitably has repercussions in the sphere of "praxis," that is, in our behavior and also in the concrete experience of values. In fact, he who accepts the ethos of the enunciation of Matthew 5:27-28 must know that he is also *called to full and mature spontaneity* of the relations that spring from the perennial attraction of masculinity and femininity. This very spontaneity is the gradual fruit of the discernment of the impulses of one's own heart.

NEED TO BE AWARE

3. Christ's words are severe. They demand from man that, in the sphere in which relations with persons of the other sex are formed, he should have full and deep consciousness of his own acts, and above all of interior acts; that he

should be aware of the internal impulses of his "heart," so as to be able to distinguish them and qualify them maturely. Christ's words demand that in this sphere, which seems to belong exclusively to the body and to the senses, that is, to exterior man, he should succeed in being really an interior man; that he should be able to obey correct conscience; to be the true master of his own deep impulses, like a guardian who watches over a hidden spring; and finally to draw from all those impulses what is fitting for "purity of heart," building with conscience and consistency that personal sense of the nuptial meaning of the body, which opens the interior space of the freedom of the gift.

LEARNING REACTIONS
OF HIS OWN HEART

4. Well, if man wishes to respond to the call expressed by Matthew 5:27-28, he must learn, with perseverance and consistency, what is the meaning of the body, the meaning of femininity and masculinity. He must learn this not only through an objectivizing abstraction (although this, too, is necessary), but above all in the sphere of the interior reactions of his own "heart." This is a "science," which cannot really be learned only from books, because it is a question here in the first place of deep "knowledge" of human interiority. In the sphere of this knowledge, man learns to distinguish between what, on the one hand, composes the multiform

riches of masculinity and femininity in the signs that come from their perennial call and creative attraction, and what, on the other hand, bears only the sign of lust. And although these variants and nuances of the internal movements of the "heart" can, within a certain limit, be confused with one another, it must be said, however, that interior man has been called by Christ to acquire a mature and complete evaluation, leading him to discern and judge the various movements of his very heart. And it should be added that this task *can* be carried out and is really worthy of man.

In fact, the discernment of which we are speaking has an essential relationship with spontaneity. The subjective structure of man shows, in this area, a specific richness and a clear distinction. Consequently, a noble gratification, for example, is one thing, while sexual desire is another; when sexual desire is linked with a noble gratification, it differs from desire pure and simple. Similarly, as regards the sphere of the immediate reactions of the "heart," sexual excitement is very different from the deep emotion with which not only interior sensitivity, but sexuality itself reacts to the total expression of femininity and masculinity. It is not possible here to develop this subject further. But it is certain that, if we affirm that Christ's words according to Matthew 5:27-28 are severe, they are also severe in the sense that they contain within them the deep requirements concerning human spontaneity.

AT THE PRICE OF SELF-CONTROL

5. There cannot be such spontaneity in all the movements and impulses that arise from mere carnal lust, devoid as it is of a choice and of an adequate hierarchy. It is precisely at the price of self-control that man reaches that deeper and more mature spontaneity with which his "heart," mastering his instincts, rediscovers the spiritual beauty of the sign constituted by the human body in its masculinity and femininity. Since this discovery is enhanced in the conscience as conviction, and in the will as guidance both of possible choices and of mere desires, the human heart becomes a participant, so to speak, in another spontaneity, of which "carnal man" knows nothing or very little. There is no doubt that through Christ's words according to Matthew 5:27-28, we are called precisely to such spontaneity. And perhaps the most important sphere of "praxis" —concerning the more "interior" acts—is precisely that which gradually prepares the way towards such spontaneity.

This is a vast subject which it will be opportune for us to take up another time in the future, when we will dedicate ourselves to showing what is the real nature of the evangelical "purity of heart." We conclude for the present saying that the words of the Sermon on the Mount, with which Christ calls the attention of His listeners—at that time and today—to "lust" ("looking lustfully"), indirectly indicate the way towards a mature spontaneity of the human "heart," which does not suffocate its noble desires and aspirations, but, on the contrary, frees them and, in a way, facilitates them.

Let what we said about the mutual relationship between what is "ethical" and what is "erotic," according to the ethos of the Sermon on the Mount, suffice for the present.

Christ Calls Us To Rediscover the Living Forms of the New Man

General audience of December 3, 1980.

1. At the beginning of our considerations on Christ's words in the Sermon on the Mount (Mt. 5:27-28), we saw that they contain a deep ethical and anthropological meaning. It is a question here of the passage in which Christ recalls the commandment: "You shall not commit adultery," and adds: "Everyone who looks at a woman lustfully has already committed adultery with her in his heart." We speak of the ethical and anthropological meaning of these words, because they allude to the two closely connected dimensions of ethos and "historical" man. In the course of the preceding analyses, we tried to follow these two dimensions, always keeping in mind that Christ's words are addressed to the "heart," that is, to interior man. Interior man is the specific subject of the ethos of the body, with which Christ wishes to imbue the conscience and will of His listeners and disciples. It is certainly a "new" ethos. It is "new," in comparison with the ethos of Old

Testament men, as we have already tried to show in more detailed analyses. It is "new" also with regard to the state of "historical" man, subsequent to original sin, that is, with regard to the "man of lust." It is, therefore, a "new" ethos in a universal sense and significance. It is "new" in relation to any man, independently of any geographical and historical longitude and latitude.

TOWARDS THE REDEMPTION OF THE BODY

2. We have on several occasions already called this "new" ethos, which emerges from the perspective of Christ's words spoken in the Sermon on the Mount, the "ethos of redemption" and, more precisely, the ethos of the redemption of the body. Here we followed Saint Paul, who in the Letter to the Romans contrasts "bondage to decay" (Rom. 8:21) and submission "to futility" (ibid., 8:20)—in which the whole of creation has become participant owing to sin—with the desire for "the redemption of our bodies" (ibid., 8:23). In this context, the Apostle speaks of the groans "of the whole creation," which "waits with eager longing..." to "be set free from its bondage to decay and obtain the glorious liberty of the children of God" (ibid., 8:20-21). In this way, St. Paul reveals the situation of all creation, and in particular that of man after sin. Significant for this situation is the aspiration which—together with the new "adoption as sons" (ibid., 8:23)—

strives precisely towards "the redemption of the body," which is presented as the end, the eschatological and mature fruit of the mystery of the redemption of man and of the world, carried out by Christ.

PERSPECTIVE OF REDEMPTION ALONE JUSTIFIES

3. In what sense, therefore, can we speak of the ethos of redemption and especially of the ethos of the redemption of the body? We must recognize that in the context of the words of the Sermon on the Mount (Mt. 5:27-28), which we have analyzed, this meaning does not yet appear in all its fullness. It will be manifested more completely when we examine other words of Christ, the ones, that is, in which He refers to the resurrection (cf. Mt. 22:30; Mk. 12:25; Lk. 20:35-36). However, there is no doubt that also in the Sermon on the Mount, Christ speaks in the perspective of the redemption of man and of the world (and, therefore, precisely of the "redemption of the body"). This is, in fact, the perspective of the whole Gospel, of the whole teaching, in fact of the whole mission of Christ. And although the immediate context of the Sermon on the Mount indicates the law and the prophets as the historical reference point, characteristic of the People of God of the Old Covenant, yet we can never forget that in Christ's teaching the fundamental reference to the question of marriage and the problem of the

relations between man and woman, refers to "the beginning." Such a reference can be justified only by the reality of the redemption; outside it, in fact, there would remain solely the three forms of lust or that "bondage to decay," of which the Apostle Paul writes (Rom. 8:21). Only the perspective of the redemption justifies the reference to the "beginning," that is, the perspective of the mystery of creation in the totality of Christ's teaching on the problems of marriage, man and woman and their mutual relationship. The words of Matthew 5:27-28 are set, in a word, in the same theological perspective.

REDISCOVERING WHAT IS TRULY HUMAN

4. In the Sermon on the Mount Christ does not invite man to return to the state of original innocence, because humanity has irrevocably left it behind, but He calls him to rediscover—on the foundation of the perennial and, so to speak, indestructible meanings of what is "human" —the living forms of the "new man." In this way a link, or rather a continuity is established between the "beginning" and the perspective of redemption. In the ethos of the redemption of the body, the original ethos of creation will have to be taken up again. Christ does not change the law, but confirms the commandment: "You shall not commit adultery"; but, at the same time, He leads the intellect and the heart of

listeners toward that "fullness of justice" willed by God the Creator and Legislator, that this commandment contains. This fullness is discovered: first with an interior view "of the heart," and then with an adequate way of being and acting. The form of the "new man" can emerge from this way of being and acting, to the extent to which the ethos of the redemption of the body dominates the lust of the flesh and the whole man of lust. Christ clearly indicates that the way to attain this must be the way of temperance and mastery of desires, that is, at the very root, already in the purely interior sphere ("Everyone who looks at a woman lustfully..."). The ethos of redemption contains in every area—and directly in the sphere of the lust of the flesh—the imperative of self-control, the necessity of immediate continence and of habitual temperance.

REALIZED THROUGH
SELF-MASTERY

5. However, temperance and continence do not mean—if it may be put in this way—suspension in emptiness: neither in the emptiness of values nor in the emptiness of the subject. The ethos of redemption is realized in self-mastery, by means of temperance, that is, continence of desires. In this behavior the human heart remains bound to the value from which, through desire, it would otherwise have moved away, turning towards pure lust deprived

of ethical value (as we said in the preceding analysis). In the field of the ethos of redemption, union with that value by means of an act of mastery, is confirmed or re-established with an even deeper power and firmness. And it is a question here of the value of the nuptial meaning of the body, of the value of a transparent sign, by means of which the Creator—together with the perennial mutual attraction of man and woman through masculinity and femininity—has written in the heart of both the gift of communion, that is, the mysterious reality of His image and likeness. It is a question of this value in the act of self-mastery and temperance, to which Christ refers in the Sermon on the Mount (Mt. 5:27-28).

EXPERIENCING FREEDOM

6. This act may give the impression of suspension "in the emptiness of the subject." It may give this impression particularly when it is necessary to make up one's mind to carry it out for the first time, or, even more, when the opposite habit has been formed, when man is accustomed to yield to the lust of the flesh. However, even the first time, and all the more so if he then acquires the capacity, man already gradually experiences his own dignity and, by means of temperance, bears witness to his own self-mastery and shows that he is carrying out what is essentially personal in him. And, furthermore, he gradually experiences the freedom of the gift, which in one way is the condition, and

in another way is the response of the subject to the nuptial value of the human body, in its femininity and its masculinity. In this way, therefore, the ethos of the redemption of the body is realized through self-mastery, through the temperance of "desires," when the human heart enters into an alliance with this ethos, or rather confirms it by means of its own integral subjectivity: when the deepest and yet most real possibilities and dispositions of the person are manifested, when the innermost layers of his potentiality acquire a voice, layers which the lust of the flesh, so to speak, would not permit to show themselves. Nor can these layers emerge when the human heart is bound in permanent suspicion, as is the case in Freudian hermeneutics. Nor can they be manifested when the Manichaean "anti-value" is dominant in consciousness. The ethos of redemption, on the other hand, is based on a close alliance with those layers.

PURITY—A REQUIREMENT

7. Further reflections will give us other proofs. Concluding our analyses on Christ's significant enunciation according to Matthew 5:27-28, we see that in it the human "heart" is above all the object of a call and not of an accusation. At the same time, we must admit that the consciousness of sinfulness is, in "historical" man, not only a necessary starting point, but also an indispensable condition of his

aspiration to virtue, to "purity of heart," to perfection. The ethos of the redemption of the body remains deeply rooted in the anthropological and axiological realism of revelation. Referring, in this case, to the "heart," Christ formulates His words in the most concrete way: man, in fact, is unique and unrepeatable above all because of his "heart," which decides his being "from within." The category of the "heart" is, in a way, the equivalent of personal subjectivity. The way of appeal to purity of heart, as it was expressed in the Sermon on the Mount, is in any case a reminiscence of the original solitude, from which the male-man was liberated through opening to the other human being, woman. Purity of heart is explained, finally, with regard for the other subject, who is originally and perennially "co-called."

Purity is a requirement of love. It is the dimension of its interior truth in man's "heart."

Purity of Heart

General audience of December 10, 1980

1. The analysis of purity is an indispensable completion of the words spoken by Christ in the Sermon on the Mount, on which the cycle of our present reflections is centered. When Christ, explaining the correct meaning of the commandment, "You shall not commit adultery," appealed to the interior man, He specified at the same time the fundamental dimension of purity that marks the mutual relations between man and woman both in marriage and outside it. The words: "But I say to you that every one who looks at a woman lustfully has already committed adultery with her in his heart" (Mt. 5:27-28), express what is opposed to purity. At the same time, these words demand the purity which, in the Sermon on the Mount, is included in the list of the beatitudes: "Blessed are the pure in heart, for they shall see God" (Mt. 5:8). In this way Christ makes an appeal to the human heart: He calls upon it, He does not accuse it, as we have already clarified previously.

RITUAL ABLUTIONS

2. Christ sees in the heart, in man's inner self, the source of purity—but also of moral

198

impurity—in the fundamental and most generic sense of the word. That is confirmed, for example, by the answer given to the Pharisees, who were scandalized by the fact that His disciples "transgress the tradition of the elders. For they do not wash their hands when they eat" (Mt. 15:2). Jesus then said to those present: "Not what goes into the mouth defiles a man, but what comes out of the mouth, this defiles a man" (Mt. 15:11). To His disciples, on the other hand, answering Peter's question, He explained these words as follows: "...what comes out of the mouth proceeds from the heart, and this defiles a man. For out of the heart come evil thoughts, murder, adultery, fornication, theft, false witness, slander. These are what defile a man; but to eat with unwashed hands does not defile a man" (cf. Mt. 15:18-20; also Mk. 7:20-23).

When we say "purity," "pure," in the first meaning of these words, we indicate what is in contrast with dirty. "To dirty" means " to make filthy," "to pollute." That refers to the various spheres of the physical world. We talk, for example, of a "dirty road," a "dirty room"; we talk also of "polluted air." In the same way also man can be "filthy," when his body is not clean. To remove the dirt of the body, it must be washed.

In the Old Testament tradition, great importance was attributed to ritual ablutions, e.g., to wash one's hands before eating, of which the above-mentioned text speaks.

Numerous and detailed prescriptions concerned the ablutions of the body in relation to sexual impurity, understood in the exclusively physiological sense, to which we have referred previously (cf. Lv. 15). According to the state of the medical science of the time, the various ablutions may have corresponded to hygienic prescriptions. Since they were imposed in God's name and contained in the Sacred Books of the Old Testament legislation, observance of them acquired, indirectly, a religious meaning; they were ritual ablutions and, in the life of the man of the Old Covenant, they served ritual "purity."

PURITY IN THE MORAL SENSE

3. In relation to the aforesaid juridico-religious tradition of the Old Covenant, there developed an erroneous way of understanding moral purity.[1] It was often taken in the exclusively exterior and "material" sense. In any case, an explicit tendency to this interpretation spread. Christ opposes it radically: Nothing "from outside" makes man filthy, no "material" dirt makes man impure in the moral, that is, interior sense. No ablution, not even of a ritual nature, is capable in itself of producing moral purity. This has its exclusive source within man: it comes from the heart.

It is probable that the respective prescriptions in the Old Testament (those, for example, that are found in Leviticus 15:16-24; 18:1ff., or 12:1-5) served, in addition to hygienic purposes, also to attribute a certain dimension of interiority to what is corporeal and sexual in the human person. In any case, Christ took good care not to connect purity in the moral (ethical) sense with physiology and its organic proc- esses. In the light of the words of Matthew 15:18-20, quoted above, none of the aspects of sexual "dirtiness," in the strictly bodily, bio- physiological sense, falls by itself into the defi- nition of purity or impurity in the moral (ethical) sense.

A GENERAL CONCEPT

4. The aforesaid assertion (Mt. 15:18-20) is important above all for semantic reasons. Speaking of purity in the moral sense, that is, of the virtue of purity, we make use of an analogy, according to which moral evil is compared pre- cisely to uncleanness. Certainly this analogy has been a part of the sphere of ethical concepts from the most remote times. Christ takes it up again and confirms it in all its extension: "What comes out of the mouth proceeds from the heart, and this defiles a man." Here Christ speaks of all moral evil, of all sin, that is, of transgressions of the various commandments, and He enumerates "evil thoughts, murder, adultery, fornication, theft, false witness, slan- der," without confining Himself to a specific kind of sin. It follows that the concept of "pu- rity" and "impurity" in the moral sense is in the first place a general concept, not a specific

one: so that all moral good is a manifestation of purity, and all moral evil is a manifestation of impurity.

The statement of Matthew 15:18-20 does not limit purity to one area of morality, namely, to the one connected with the commandment: "You shall not commit adultery" and "Do not covet your neighbor's wife," that is, to the one that concerns the mutual relations between man and woman, linked to the body and to the relative concupiscence. Similarly we can also understand the beatitude of the Sermon on the Mount, addressed to "the pure in heart," both in the general and in the more specific sense. Only the actual context will make it possible to delimit and clarify this meaning.

THE FLESH AND THE SPIRIT

5. The wider and more general meaning of purity is present also in St. Paul's letters, in which we shall gradually pick out the contexts which explicitly limit the meaning of purity to the "bodily" and "sexual" sphere, that is, to that meaning which we can grasp from the words of Christ in the Sermon on the Mount on lust, which is already expressed in "looking at a woman," and is regarded as equivalent to "committing adultery in one's heart" (cf. Mt. 5:27-28).

It is not St. Paul who is the author of the words about the three forms of lust. They occur, as we know, in the First Letter of John. It can be said, however, that similarly to what is for John (1 Jn. 2:16-17) the opposition within man between God and the world (between what comes "from the Father" and what comes "from the world")—an opposition which is born in the heart and penetrates into man's actions as "the lust of the flesh and the lust of the eyes and the pride of life"—St. Paul points out another contradiction in the Christian. It is the opposition and at the same time the tension between the "flesh" and the "Spirit" (written with a capital letter, that is, the Holy Spirit): "But I say, walk by the Spirit, and do not gratify the desires of the flesh. For the desires of the flesh are against the Spirit, and the desires of the Spirit are against the flesh; for these are opposed to each other, to prevent you from doing what you would" (Gal. 5:16-17). It follows that life "according to the flesh" is in opposition to life "according to the Spirit." "For those who live according to the flesh set their minds on the things of the flesh, but those who live according to the Spirit set their minds on the things of the Spirit" (Rom. 8:5).

In subsequent analyses we shall seek to show that purity—the purity of heart of which Christ spoke in the Sermon on the Mount—is realized precisely in life "according to the Spirit."

FOOTNOTE

1. Alongside a complex system of prescriptions concerning ritual purity, on which legal casuistry was based, there also existed in the Old Testament the concept of moral purity. It was handed down by means of two channels.

The *Prophets* demanded behavior in conformity with God's will, which presupposes conversion of heart, interior obedience and complete uprightness before Him (cf. for example Is. 1:10-20; Jer. 4:14; 24:7; Ez. 36:25ff.). A similar attitude is required also by the Psalmist:

"Who shall ascend the hill of the Lord... / He who has clean hands and a pure heart... / will receive blessing from the Lord" (Ps. 24/23:3-5).

According to *the priestly tradition,* man is aware of his deep sinfulness and, not being able to purify himself by his own power, he beseeches God to bring about this change of heart, which can only be the work of a creative act of His:

"Create in me a clean heart, O God... / wash me, and I shall be whiter than snow... / a broken and contrite heart, O God, you will not despise" (Ps. 51/50:10, 7, 17).

Both Old Testament channels meet in the beatitude of the "pure in heart" (Mt. 5:8), even if its verbal formulation seems to be closer to Psalm 24 (cf. J. Dupont, *Les Béatitudes,* vol. III; *Les Evangélistes,* Paris 1973, Gabalda, pp. 603-604).

Justification in Christ

General audience of December 17, 1980.

1. "The desires of the flesh are against the Spirit, and the desires of the Spirit are against the flesh." Today we wish to study further these words of St. Paul in the Letter to the Galatians (5:17), with which we ended our reflections last week on the subject of the correct meaning of purity. Paul has in mind the tension existing within man, precisely in his "heart." It is not a question here only of the body (matter) and of the spirit (the soul), as of two essentially different anthropological elements which constitute from the "beginning" the very essence of man. But that disposition of forces formed in man with original sin, in which every "historical" man participates, is presupposed. In this disposition, formed within man, the body opposes the spirit and easily prevails over it.[1] The Pauline terminology, however, means something more: here the prevalence of the "flesh" seems almost to coincide with what, according to Johannine terminology, is the threefold lust "of the world." The "flesh," in the language of St. Paul's letters,[2] indicates not only the "exterior" man, but also the man who is "interiorly" subjected to the "world;"[3]

closed, in a way, in the area of those values that belong only to the world and of those ends that it is capable of imposing on man: values, therefore, to which man as "flesh" is sensitive. Thus Paul's language seems to link up with the essential contents of John, and the language of both denotes what is defined by various terms of modern ethics and anthropology, such as, for example: "humanistic autarchy," "secularism" or also, in a general sense, "sensualism." The man who lives "according to the flesh" is the man ready only for what is "of the world": he is the man of the "senses," the man of the three-fold lust. His actions confirm this, as we shall say shortly.

WHAT THE SPIRIT WANTS

2. This man lives almost at the opposite pole as compared with what "the Spirit wants." The Spirit of God wants a different reality from the one desired by the flesh; He aspires to a different reality from the one to which the flesh aspires, and that already within man, already at the interior source of man's aspirations and actions—"to prevent you from doing what you would" (Gal. 5:17).

Paul expresses that in an even more explicit way, writing elsewhere of the evil he does, though he does not want to do so, and of the impossibility—or rather the limited possibility—of carrying out the good he "wants" (cf. Rom. 7:19). Without going into the problems of a detailed exegesis of this text, it could be said that the tension between the "flesh" and the "spirit" is, first, immanent, even if it is not reduced to this level. It is manifested in his heart as a "fight" between good and evil. That desire, of which Christ speaks in the Sermon on the Mount (cf. Mt. 5:27-28), although it is an "interior" act, is certainly—according to Pauline language—a manifestation of life, "according to the flesh." At the same time, that desire enables us to see how, within man, life "according to the flesh" is opposed to life "according to the Spirit," and how the latter, in man's present state, in view of his hereditary sinfulness, is constantly exposed to the weakness and insufficiency of the former, to which it often yields, if it is not strengthened interiorly to do precisely what "the Spirit wants." We can deduce from this that Paul's words, which deal with life "according to the flesh" and "according to the Spirit," are at the same time a synthesis and a program; and it is necessary to understand them in this key.

ST. PAUL EXPLAINS
THIS OPPOSITION

3. We find the same opposition of life "according to the flesh" and life "according to the Spirit" in the Letter to the Romans. Here too (as moreover in the Letter to the Galatians) it is placed in the context of Pauline doctrine on justification by means of faith, that is, by means of the power of Christ Himself operating within

man by means of the Holy Spirit. In this context
Paul takes that opposition to its extreme consequences when he writes: "Those who live according to the flesh set their minds on the
things of the flesh, but those who live according
to the Spirit set their minds on the things of the
Spirit. To set the mind on the flesh is death, but
to set the mind on the Spirit is life and peace.
For the mind that is set on the flesh is hostile to
God; it does not submit to God's law, indeed it
cannot; and those who are in the flesh cannot
please God. But you are not in the flesh, you are
in the Spirit, if in fact the Spirit of God dwells
in you. Anyone who does not have the Spirit of
Christ does not belong to him. But if Christ is in
you, although your bodies are dead because of
sin, your spirits are alive because of righteousness " (Rom. 8:5-10).

FINAL VICTORY OVER SIN AND DEATH

4. The horizons that Paul delineates in this
text can clearly be seen: he goes back to the
"beginning"—that is, in this case, to the first
sin from which life "according to the flesh"
originated and which created in man the heritage of a predisposition to live only such a life,
together with the legacy of death. At the same
time Paul anticipates the final victory over sin
and over death, of which the resurrection of
Christ is a sign and announcement: "He who
raised Christ Jesus from the dead will give life
to your mortal bodies also through his Spirit

which dwells in you" (Rom. 8:11). And in this eschatological perspective, St. Paul stresses justification in Christ, already intended for "historical" man, for every man of "yesterday, today and tomorrow" in the history of the world and also in the history of salvation: a justification which is essential for interior man, and is destined precisely for that "heart" to which Christ appealed, when speaking of "purity" and "impurity" in the moral sense. This "justification" by faith is not just a dimension of the divine plan of man's salvation and sanctification, but is, according to St. Paul, a real power that operates in man and is revealed and asserts itself in his actions.

WORKS OF THE FLESH

5. Here again are the words of the Letter to the Galatians: "Now the works of the flesh are plain: fornication, impurity, licentiousness, idolatry, sorcery, enmity, strife, jealousy, anger, selfishness, dissension, party spirit, envy, drunkenness, carousing, and the like..." (5:19-21). "But the fruit of the Spirit is love, joy, peace, patience, kindness, goodness, faithfulness, gentleness, self-control..." (5:22-23). In the Pauline doctrine, life "according to the flesh" is opposed to life "according to the Spirit" not only within man, in his "heart," but, as can be seen, it finds an ample and differentiated field to express itself in works. Paul speaks, on the one hand, of the "works" which spring from the "flesh"—it could be said: from

the works in which the man who lives "accord-ing to the flesh" is manifested—and, on the other hand, he speaks of the "fruit of the Spirit," that is of the actions,[4] of the ways of behaving, of the virtues, in which the man who lives "according to the Spirit" is manifested. While in the first case we are dealing with man abandoned to the threefold lust, of which John says that it is "of the world," in the second case we have before us what we have already previously called the ethos of redemption. Only now are we able to clarify fully the nature and structure of that ethos. It is expressed and af-firmed through what in man, in all his "operating," in actions and in behavior, is the fruit of dominion over the threefold lust: of the flesh, of the eyes, and of the pride of life (of all that the human heart can rightly be "accused" of, and of which man and his interiority can continually be "suspected").

FRUIT OF THE SPIRIT

6. If mastery in the sphere of ethos is mani-fested and realized as "love, joy, peace, patience, kindness, goodness, faithfulness, gen-tleness, self-control"—as we read in the Letter to the Galatians—then behind each of these realizations, these ways of behaving, these moral virtues, there is a specific choice, that is, an effort of the will, the fruit of the human spirit permeated by the Spirit of God, which is mani-fested in choosing good. Speaking with the lan-guage of Paul: "The desires of the Spirit are

against the flesh" (Gal. 5:17) and in these "desires" the Spirit shows Himself to be stronger than the "flesh" and the desires brought forth by threefold lust. In this struggle between good and evil, man proves himself stronger, thanks to the power of the Holy Spirit, who, operating within man's spirit, causes his desires to bear fruit in good. These, therefore, are not only—and not so much—"works" of man, as "fruit," that is, the effect of the action of the "Spirit" in man. And therefore Paul speaks of the fruit of the "Spirit," intending this word with a capital letter.

Without penetrating into the structures of human interiority by means of the subtle differentiations furnished to us by systematic theology (especially from Thomas Aquinas), we limit ourselves to a summary exposition of the biblical doctrine, which enables us to understand, in an essential and sufficient way, the distinction and the opposition of the "flesh" and the "Spirit."

We have pointed out that among the fruits of the Spirit the Apostle also puts "self-control." This must not be forgotten, because in our further reflections we will take up this subject again to deal with it in a more detailed way.

FOOTNOTES

1. "Paul never, like the Greeks, identified 'sinful flesh' with the physical body....

"Flesh, then, in Paul is not to be identified with sex or with the physical body. It is closer to the Hebrew thought of the physical personality—the self including physical and psychical elements as vehicles of the outward life and the lower levels of experience.

"It is man in his humanness with all the limitations, moral weakness, vulnerability, creatureliness and morality, which being human implies....

"Man is vulnerable both to evil and to God; he is a vehicle, a channel, a dwelling place, a temple, a battlefield (Paul uses each metaphor) for good and evil.

"Which shall possess, indwell, master him—whether sin, evil, the spirit that now worketh in the children of disobedience, or Christ, the Holy Spirit, faith, grace—it is for each man to choose.

"That he *can* so choose, brings to view the other side of Paul's conception of human nature, man's *conscience* and the human *spirit*" (R. E. O. White, Biblical Ethics, Exeter 1979, Paternoster Press, pp. 135-138).

2. The interpretation of the Greek word *sarx* "flesh" in Paul's Letters depends on the context of the Letter. In the Letter to the Galatians, for example, at least two distinct meanings of *sarx* can be specified.

Writing to the Galatians, Paul was fighting two dangers which threatened the young Christian community.

On the one hand, converts from Judaism were trying to convince converts from paganism to accept circumcision, which was obligatory in Judaism. Paul reproaches them with "wanting to make a good showing in the flesh," that is, of restoring hope in the circumcision of the flesh. So "flesh" in this context (Gal. 3:1-5, 12; 6:12-18) means "circumcision," as the symbol of a new submission to the laws of Judaism.

The second danger in the young Galatian Church came from the influence of the "Pneumatics" who understood the work of the Holy Spirit as the divinization of man rather than as a power operating in an ethical sense. That led them to underestimate moral principles. Writing to them, Paul calls "flesh" everything that brings man closer to the object of his lust and entices him with the tempting promise of a life that is apparently fuller (cf. Gal. 5:13; 6:10).

Sarx, therefore, "makes a good showing" of the "Law" as well as of its infraction, and in both cases promises what it cannot fulfill.

Paul distinguishes explicitly between the object of the action and *sarx*. The center of the decision is not in the "flesh": "Walk by the Spirit, and do not gratify the desires of the flesh" (Gal. 5:16).

Man falls into the slavery of the flesh when he trusts in the "flesh" and in what it promises (in the sense of the "Law" or of infraction of the law). (Cf. F. Mussner, *Der Galaterbrief, Herders Theolog. Kommentar zum NT*, IX, Freiburg 1974, Herder, p. 367; R. Jewett, *Paul's Anthropological Terms, A Study of Their Use in Conflict Settings, Arbeiten zur Geschichte des antiken Judentums und des Urchistentums*, X, Leiden 1971—Brill—pp. 95-106).

3. Paul stresses in his Letters the dramatic character of what is going on in the world. Since men, through their fault, have forgotten God, "therefore God gave them up in the lusts of their hearts to impurity" (Rom. 1:24), from which there also comes all moral disorder, which distorts both sexual life *(ibid.,* 1:24-27) and the operation of social and economic life *(ibid.,* 1:29-32) and even cultural life; in fact, "though they know God's decree that those who do such things deserve to die, they not only do them but approve those who practice them" *(ibid.,* 1:32).

From the moment that, through one man, sin came into the world *(ibid.,* 5:12), "the god of this world has blinded the minds of the unbelievers, to keep them from seeing the light of the gospel of the glory of Christ" (2 Cor. 4:4); and therefore too "the wrath of God is revealed from heaven against all ungodliness and wickedness of men who by their wickedness suppress the truth" (Rom. 1:1).

Therefore "the creation waits with eager longing for the revealing of the sons of God...because the creation itself will be set free from its bondage to decay and obtain the glorious liberty of the children of God" *(ibid.,* 8:19-21), that liberty for which "Christ has set us free" (Gal. 5:1).

The concept of "world" in St. John has various meanings: in his first Letter, the world is the place in which threefold lust is manifested (1 Jn. 2:15-16) and in which the false prophets and adversaries of Christ try to seduce the faithful; but Christians defeat the world thanks to their faith *(ibid.,* 5:4); the world, in fact, passes away with its lust, and he who does the will of God lives forever (cf. *ibid.,* 2:17).

(Cf. P. Grelot, *"Monde,"* in: *Dictionnaire de Spiritualité, Ascétique et mystique, doctrine et histoire*, fascicules 68-69), Beauchesne, p. 1628ff. Furthermore; J. Mateos

J. Barreto, *Vocabulario teologico del Evangelio de Juan*, Madrid 1980, Edic. Cristianidad, pp. 211-215).

4. Exegetes point out that, although for Paul the concept of "fruit" is sometimes applied also to the "works of the flesh" (e.g., Rom. 6:21; 7:5), yet "the fruit of the Spirit" is never called "work."

For Paul, in fact, "works" are the specific acts of man (or that in which Israel lays hope, without a reason), for which he will be answerable before God.

Paul also avoids the term "virtue," *arete;* it is found only once, in a very general sense, in Philippians 4:8. In the Greek world this word had a too anthropocentric meaning; the Stoics particularly stressed the self-sufficiency or *autarchy* of virtue.

On the other hand, the term "fruit of the Spirit" emphasizes God's action in man. This "fruit" grows in him like the gift of a life whose only Author is God; man can, at most, promote suitable conditions, in order that the fruit may grow and ripen.

The fruit of the Spirit, in the singular form, corresponds in some way to the "justice" of the Old Testament, which embraces the whole of life in conformity with God's will; it also corresponds, in a certain sense, to the "virtue" of the Stoics, which was indivisible. We see this, for example, in Ephesians 5:9-11: "The fruit of light is found in all that is good and right and true.... Take no part in the unfruitful works of darkness...."

However, "the fruit of the Spirit" is different both from "justice" and from "virtue," because (in all its manifestations and differentiations which are seen in the lists of virtues) it contains the effect of the action of the Spirit, which, in the Church, is the foundation and fulfillment of the Christian's life.

Cf. H. Schlier, *Der Brief an die Galater*, Meyer's Kommentar Göttingen 1971(5) Vandenhoeck-Ruprecht, pp. 255-264; O. Bauernfeind, *arete* in: *Theological Dictionary of the New Testament*, ed. G. Kittel, G. Bromley, vol. 1, Grand Rapids 1978(9), Eerdmans, p. 460; W. Tatarkiewicz, *Historia Filozofii, t.1. Warszawa 1970, PWN p. 121;* E. Kamlah, *Die Form der katalogischen Paränese im Neuen Testament*, Wissenschaftliche Untersuchungen zum Neuen Testament, 7, Tübingen 1964, Mhr, p. 14).

Opposition Between
the Flesh and the Spirit

General audience of January 7, 1981.

Dearest brothers in the episcopate, in the priesthood, brothers and sisters in religious life, and all you dearest brothers and sisters:

After the pause due to the recent feasts, we resume today our Wednesday meetings. We still carry in our hearts the serene joy of the mystery of Christ's birth which the Church's liturgy in this period has led us to celebrate and put into effect in our lives. Jesus of Nazareth, the Child cradled in the manger of Bethlehem, is the eternal Word of God who became Incarnate for love of man (Jn. 1:14). This is the great truth to which the Christian adheres with profound faith. With the faith of Mary most holy, who, in the glory of her intact virginity conceived and brought forth the Son of God made man. With the faith of St. Joseph who guarded and protected him with immense dedication of love. With the faith of the shepherds who hastened immediately to the cave of the nativity. With the faith of the Magi who glimpsed Him in the sign of the star, and who, after a long search, were able to contemplate and adore Him in the arms of the Virgin Mary.

May the new year be lived by all under the sign of this great interior joy, the fruit of the certainty that God has so loved the world as to give His only-begotten Son, that he who believes in Him should not die but should have eternal life.

That is the wish which I address to all of you present at this first general audience of 1981, and to all your dear ones.

PAULINE THEOLOGY OF JUSTIFICATION

1. What does the statement mean: "The desires of the flesh are against the Spirit, and the desires of the Spirit are against the flesh"? (Gal. 5:17) This question seems important, even fundamental, in the context of our reflections on purity of heart, of which the Gospel speaks. However, the author of the Letter to the Galatians opens up before us, in this regard, even wider horizons. In this contrast between the "flesh" and the Spirit (Spirit of God), and between life "according to the flesh" and life "according to the Spirit," there is contained the Pauline theology about justification, that is, the expression of faith in the anthropological and ethical realism of the redemption carried out by Christ, which Paul, in the context already known to us, also calls "redemption of the body." According to the Letter to the Romans 8:23, the "redemption of the body" has also a "cosmic" dimension (referred to the whole of creation), but at its center there is man: man

constituted in the personal unity of spirit and body. It is precisely in this man, in his "heart," and consequently in all his behavior, that Christ's redemption bears fruit, thanks to those powers of the Spirit which bring about "justification," that is, which enable justice "to abound" in man, as is inculcated in the Sermon on the Mount (Mt. 5:20), that is, "to abound" to the extent that God Himself willed and which He expects.

EFFECTS OF THE LUST OF THE FLESH

2. It is significant that Paul, speaking of the "works of the flesh" (cf. Gal. 5:19-21), mentions not only "fornication, impurity, licentiousness...drunkenness, carousing"—therefore everything that, according to an objective way of understanding, takes on the character of "carnal sins" and of the sensual enjoyment connected with the flesh—but he names other sins too, to which we would not be inclined to attribute also a "carnal" and "sensual" character: "idolatry, sorcery, enmity, strife, jealousy, anger, selfishness, dissension, party spirit, envy..." (Gal. 5:20-21). According to our anthropological (and ethical) categories we would rather be inclined to call all the "works" listed here "sins of the spirit" of man, rather than sins of the "flesh." Not without reason we might have glimpsed in them the effects of the "lust of the eyes" or of the "pride of life," rather than

the effects of the "lust of the flesh." However, Paul describes them all as "works of the flesh." That is intended exclusively against the background of that wider meaning (in a way a metonymical one), which the term "flesh" assumes in the Pauline Letters, opposed not only and not so much to the human "spirit" as to the Holy Spirit who works in man's soul (spirit).

PURITY COMES FROM THE HEART

3. There exists, therefore, a significant analogy between what Paul defines as "works of the flesh" and the words with which Christ explains to His disciples what He had previously said to the Pharisees about ritual "purity" and "impurity" (cf. Mt. 15:2-20). According to Christ's words, real "purity" (as also "impurity") in the moral sense is in the "heart" and comes "from the heart" of man. As "impure works" in the same sense, there are defined not only "adultery" and "fornication," and so the "sins of the flesh" in the strict sense, but also "evil thoughts...theft, false witness, slander." Christ, as we have already been able to note, uses here both the general and the specific meaning of "impurity" (and, therefore, indirectly also of "purity"). St. Paul expresses himself in a similar way: the works "of the flesh" are understood in the Pauline text both in the general and in the specific sense. All sins are an expression of "life according to the flesh," which is in contrast with "life according to the Spirit." What is considered, in conformity

with our linguistic convention (which is, more-over, partially justified), as a "sin of the flesh," is, in Paul's list, one of the many manifestations (or species) of what he calls "works of the flesh," and, in this sense, one of the symptoms, that is, actualizations of life "according to the flesh," and not "according to the Spirit."

TWO MEANINGS OF DEATH

4. Paul's words written to the Romans: "So then, brothers, we are debtors, not to the flesh, to live according to the flesh; for if you live according to the flesh you will die, but if by the Spirit you put to death the deeds of the body you will live" (Rom. 8:12-13)—introduce us again into the rich and differentiated sphere of the meanings which the terms "body" and "spirit" have for him. However, the definitive meaning of that enunciation is advisory, exhor-tative, and so valid for the evangelical ethos. Paul, when he speaks of the necessity of putting to death the deeds of the body with the help of the Spirit, expresses precisely what Christ spoke about in the Sermon on the Mount, appealing to the human heart and exhorting it to control desires, even those expressed in a man's "look" at a woman for the purpose of satisfying the lust of the flesh. This mastery, or, as Paul writes, "putting to death the works of the body with the help of the Spirit," is an indis-pensable condition of "life according to the Spirit," that is, of the "life" which is an anti-

thesis of the "death" spoken about in the same context. Life "according to the flesh" has, in fact, "death" as its fruit, that is, it involves as its effect the "death" of the Spirit.

So the term "death" does not mean only the death of the body, but also sin, which moral theology will call "mortal." In the Letters to the Romans and to the Galatians, the Apostle continually widens the horizon of "sin-death," both towards the "beginning" of man's history, and towards its end. And, therefore, after listing the multiform "works of the flesh," he affirms that "those who do such things shall not inherit the kingdom of God" (Gal. 5:21). Elsewhere he will write with similar firmness: "Be sure of this, that no fornicator or impure man, or one who is covetous (that is, an idolater), has any inheritance in the kingdom of God" (Eph. 5:5). In this case, too, the works that exclude "inheritance in the kingdom of Christ and of God"—that is, the "works of the flesh"—are listed as an example and with general value, although sins against "purity" in the specific sense are at the top of the list here (cf. Eph. 5:3-7).

TO SET US FREE

5. To complete the picture of the opposition between the "body" and the "fruit of the Spirit"—it should be observed that in everything that is a manifestation of life and behavior according to the Spirit, Paul sees at once the manifestation of that freedom for which Christ

"has set us free" (Gal. 5:1). In fact, he writes precisely: "For you were called to freedom, brethren; only do not use your freedom as an opportunity for the flesh, but through love be servants of one another. For the whole law is fulfilled in one word, 'You shall love your neighbor as yourself'" (Gal. 5:13-14). As we already pointed out previously, the opposition "body/Spirit," life "according to the flesh"/life "according to the Spirit," deeply permeates the whole Pauline doctrine on justification. The Apostle of the Gentiles, with exceptional force of conviction, proclaims that man's justification is carried out in Christ and through Christ. Man obtains justification in "faith working through love" (Gal. 5:6), and not only by means of the observance of the individual prescriptions of Old Testament law (in particular, that of circumcision). Justification comes therefore "from the Spirit" (of God) and not "from the flesh." He, therefore, exhorts the recipients of his Letter to free themselves of the erroneous "carnal" concept of justification, to follow the true one, that is, the "spiritual" one. In this sense he exhorts them to consider themselves free from the law, and even more to be free with the freedom for which Christ "has set us free."

In this way, therefore, following the Apostle's thought, we should consider and above all realize evangelical purity, that is, the purity of the heart, according to the measure of that freedom for which Christ "has set us free."

Life in the Spirit
Based on True Freedom

General audience of January 14, 1981.

1. St. Paul writes in the Letter to the Galatians: "For you were called to freedom, brethren; only do not use your freedom as an opportunity for the flesh, but through love be servants of one another. For the whole law is fulfilled in one word, 'You shall love your neighbor as yourself'" (Gal. 5:13-14). We have already dwelled on this enunciation a week ago; however, we are taking it up again today, in connection with the main argument of our reflections.

Although the passage quoted refers above all to the subject of justification, here, however, the Apostle aims explicitly at driving home the ethical dimension of the "body-Spirit" opposition, that is, the opposition between life according to the flesh and life according to the Spirit. Precisely here, in fact, he touches the essential point, revealing, as it were, the very anthropological roots of the Gospel ethos. If, in fact, "the whole law" (moral law of the Old Testament) "is fulfilled" in the commandment of charity, the dimension of the new Gospel ethos is nothing but an appeal to human freedom, an appeal to its fuller implementation and, in a way, to fuller "utilization" of the potential of the human spirit.

FREEDOM LINKED
WITH COMMAND TO LOVE

2. It might seem that Paul was only contrasting freedom with the law and the law with freedom. However, a deeper analysis of the text shows that St. Paul in the Letter to the Galatians emphasizes above all the ethical subordination of freedom to that element in which the whole law is fulfilled, that is, to love, which is the content of the greatest commandment of the Gospel. "Christ set us free in order that we might remain free," precisely in the sense that He manifested to us the ethical (and theological) subordination of freedom to charity, and that He linked freedom with the commandment of love. To understand the vocation to freedom in this way ("You were called to freedom, brethren": Gal 5:13), means giving a form to the ethos in which life "according to the Spirit" is realized. There also exists, in fact, the danger of understanding freedom wrongly, and Paul clearly points this out, writing in the same context: "Only do not use your freedom as an opportunity for the flesh, but through love be servants of one another" *(ibid.).*

BAD USE OF FREEDOM

3. In other words: Paul warns us of the possibility of making a bad use of freedom, a use which is in opposition to the liberation of the human spirit carried out by Christ and

which contradicts that freedom with which "Christ set us free." In fact, Christ realized and manifested the freedom that finds its fullness in charity, the freedom thanks to which we are "servants of one another." In other words: the freedom that becomes a source of new "works" and "life" according to the Spirit. The antithesis and, in a way, the negation of this use of freedom takes place when it becomes for man "a pretext to live according to the flesh." Freedom then becomes a source of "works" and of "life" according to the flesh. It stops being the true freedom for which "Christ set us free," and becomes "an opportunity for the flesh," a source (or instrument) of a specific "yoke" on the part of pride of life, the lust of the eyes, and the lust of the flesh. Anyone who in this way lives "according to the flesh," that is, submits— although in a way that is not quite conscious, but nevertheless actual—to the three forms of lust, and in particular to the lust of the flesh, ceases to be capable of that freedom for which "Christ set us free"; he also ceases to be suitable for the real gift of himself, which is the fruit and expression of this freedom. He ceases, moreover, to be capable of that gift which is organically connected with the nuptial meaning of the human body, with which we dealt in the preceding analyses of the Book of Genesis (cf. Gn. 2:23-25).

THE LAW FULFILLED

4. In this way, the Pauline doctrine on purity, a doctrine in which we find the faithful and

true echo of the Sermon on the Mount, permits us to see evangelical and Christian "purity of heart" in a wider perspective, and above all permits us to link it with the charity in which "the law is fulfilled." Paul, in a way similar to Christ, knows a double meaning of "purity" (and of "impurity"): a generic meaning and a specific meaning. In the first case, everything that is morally good is "pure," everything that is morally bad is, on the contrary, "impure." Christ's words according to Matthew 15:18-20, quoted previously, affirm this clearly. In Paul's enunciations about the "works of the flesh," which he contrasts with the "fruit of the Spirit," we find the basis for a similar way of understanding this problem. Among the "works of the flesh" Paul puts what is morally bad, while every moral good is linked with life "according to the Spirit." In this way, one of the manifestations of life "according to the Spirit" is behavior in conformity with that virtue which Paul, in the Letter to the Galatians, seems to define rather indirectly, but of which he speaks directly in the First Letter to the Thessalonians.

VIRTUE OF SELF-CONTROL

5.   In the passages of the Letter to the Galatians, which we have previously already submitted to detailed analysis, the Apostle lists in the first place among the "works of the flesh": "fornication, impurity, licentiousness." Subsequently, however, when he contrasts with these works the "fruit of the Spirit," he does not

speak directly of "purity," but names only self-control, *enkrateia*. This "control" can be recognized as a virtue which concerns continence in the area of all the desires of the senses, especially in the sexual sphere. It is, therefore, in opposition to "fornication, impurity, licentiousness," and also to "drunkenness," "carousing." It could, therefore, be admitted that Pauline "self-control" contains what is expressed in the term "continence" or "temperance," which corresponds to the Latin term *temperantia*. In this case, we would find ourselves in the presence of the well-known system of virtues which later theology, especially Scholasticism, will borrow, in a way, from the ethics of Aristotle. Paul, however, certainly does not use this system in his text. Since by "purity" must be understood the correct way of treating the sexual sphere according to one's personal state (and not necessarily absolute abstention from sexual life), then undoubtedly this "purity" is included in the Pauline concept of "self-control" or *enkrateia*. Therefore, within the Pauline text we find only a generic and indirect mention of purity; now and again the author contrasts these "works of the flesh," such as "fornication, impurity, licentiousness" with the "fruit of the Spirit"—that is, new works, in which "life according to the Spirit" is manifested. It can be deduced that one of these new works is precisely "purity": that is the one that is opposed to "impurity" and also to "fornication" and "licentiousness."

CALLED TO HOLINESS

6. But already in the First Letter to the Thessalonians, Paul writes on this subject in an explicit and unambiguous way. We read: "For this is the will of God, your sanctification: that you abstain from unchastity; that each one of you know how to control his own body[1] in holiness and honor, not in the passion of lust like heathens who do not know God" (1 Thes. 4:3-5). And then: "God has not called us for uncleanness, but in holiness. Therefore whoever disregards this, disregards not man but God, who gives his Holy Spirit to you" (1 Thes. 4:7-8). Although in this text, too, we have before us the generic meaning of "purity," identified in this case with "holiness" (since "uncleanness" is named as the antithesis of "holiness"), nevertheless the whole context indicates clearly what "purity" or "impurity" it is a question of, that is, the content of what Paul calls here "uncleanness," and in what way "purity" contributes to the "holiness" of man.

And therefore, in the following reflections, it will be useful to take up again the text of the First Letter to the Thessalonians, which has just been quoted.

FOOTNOTE

1. Without going into the detailed discussions of the exegetes, it should, however, be pointed out that the Greek expression *to heautou skeuos* can refer also to the wife (cf. 1 Pt. 3:7).

St. Paul's Teaching on the Sanctity of and Respect for the Human Body

General audience of January 28, 1981.

1. St. Paul writes in the First Letter to the Thessalonians: "...this is the will of God, your sanctification: that you abstain from unchastity, that each one of you know how to control his own body in holiness and honor, not in the passion of lust like heathens who do not know God" (1 Thes. 4:3-5). And after some verses, he continues: "God has not called us for uncleanness, but in holiness. Therefore whoever disregards this, disregards not man but God, who gives his Holy Spirit to you" *(ibid.,* 4:7-8). We referred to these sentences of the Apostle during our meeting on last January 14. We take them up again today, however, because they are particularly important for the subject of our meditations.

PURITY—A CAPACITY

2. The purity of which Paul speaks in the First Letter to the Thessalonians (4:3-5, 7-8) is manifested in the fact that man "knows how to control his own body in holiness and honor, not in the passion of lust." In this formulation every word has a particular meaning and, therefore, deserves an adequate comment.

In the first place, purity is a "capacity," that is, in the traditional language of anthropology and ethics, an aptitude. And in this sense it is a virtue. If this ability, that is, virtue, leads to abstaining "from unchastity," that happens because the man who possesses it "knows how to control his own body in holiness and honor, not in the passion of lust." It is a question here of a practical capacity which makes man capable of acting in a given way, and at the same time of not acting in the opposite way. For purity to be such a capacity or aptitude, it must obviously be rooted in the will, in the very foundation of man's willing and conscious acting. Thomas Aquinas, in his teaching on virtues, sees in an even more direct way the object of purity in the faculty of sensitive desire, which he calls *appetitus concupiscibilis*. Precisely this faculty must be particularly "mastered," subordinated and made capable of acting in a way that is in conformity with virtue, in order that "purity" may be attributed to man. According to this concept, purity consists in the first place in containing the impulse of sensitive desire, which has as its object what is corporeal and sexual in man. Purity is a different form of the virtue of temperance.

PURITY REQUIRES MASTERING

3. The text of the First Letter to the Thessalonians (4:3-5) shows that the virtue of purity, in Paul's concept, consists also in mastery and

overcoming of "the passion of lust"; that means that the capacity for controlling the impulses of sensitive desire, that is, the virtue of temperance, belongs necessarily to its nature. At the same time, however, the same Pauline text turns our attention to another role of the virtue of purity, to another of its dimensions which is, it could be said, more positive than negative. That is, the task of purity, which the author of the Letter seems to stress above all, is not only (and not so much) abstention from "unchastity" and from what leads to it, and so abstention from "the passion of lust," but, at the same time, the control of one's own body and, indirectly, also that of others, in "holiness and honor."

These two functions, "abstention" and "control," are closely connected and dependent on each other. Since, in fact, it is not possible to "control one's body in holiness and honor" if that abstention "from unchastity" and from what leads to it is lacking, it can consequently be admitted that control of one's body (and indirectly that of others) "in holiness and honor" confers adequate meaning and value on that abstention. This in itself calls for the overcoming of something that is in man and that arises spontaneously in him as an inclination, an attraction, and also as a value that acts above all in the sphere of the senses, but very often not without repercussions on the other dimensions of human subjectivity, and particularly on the affective-emotional dimension.

MANIFESTATION OF LIFE

4. Considering all this, it seems that the Pauline image of the virtue of purity—an image that emerges from the very eloquent comparison of the function of "abstention" (that is, of temperance) with that of "control of one's body in holiness and honor"—is deeply right, complete and adequate. Perhaps we owe this completeness to nothing else but the fact that Paul considers purity not only as a capacity (that is, an aptitude) of man's subjective faculties, but, at the same time, as a concrete manifestation of life "according to the Spirit," in which human capacity is interiorly made fruitful and enriched by what Paul calls, in the Letter to the Galatians 5:22, the "fruit of the Spirit." The honor that arises in man for everything that is corporeal and sexual, both in himself and in any other person, male and female, is seen to be the most essential power to control the body "in holiness." To understand the Pauline teaching on purity, it is necessary to penetrate fully the meaning of the term "honor," which is obviously understood here as a power of the spiritual order. It is precisely this interior power that confers its full dimension on purity as a virtue, that is, as the capacity of acting in that whole field in which man discovers, within himself, the multiple impulses of "the passion of lust," and sometimes, for various reasons, surrenders to them.

ABOUT THE HUMAN BODY

5. To grasp better the thought of the author of the First Letter to the Thessalonians, it will be a good thing to keep in mind also another text, which we find in the First Letter to the Corinthians. Paul sets forth in it his great ecclesiological doctrine, according to which the Church is the Body of Christ; he takes the opportunity to formulate the following argumentation about the human body: "...God arranged the organs in the body, each one of them, as he chose" (1 Cor. 12:18); and further on: "On the contrary, the parts of the body which seem to be weaker are indispensable, and those parts of the body which we think less honorable we invest with the greater honor, and our unpresentable parts are treated with greater modesty, which our more presentable parts do not require. But God has so composed the body, giving the greater honor to the inferior part, that there may be no discord in the body, but that the members may have the same care for one another" *(ibid., 12:22-25)*.

WORTHY OF HONOR

6. Although the specific subject of the text in question is the theology of the Church as the Body of Christ, it can be said, however, in connection with this passage, that Paul, by means of his great ecclesiological analogy (which recurs in other Letters, and which we will take

up again in due time), contributes, at the same time, to deepening the theology of the body. While in the First Letter to the Thessalonians he writes about control of the body "in holiness and honor," in the passage now quoted from the First Letter to the Corinthians he wishes to show this human body as, precisely, worthy of honor; it could also be said that he wishes to teach the receivers of his Letter the correct concept of the human body.

Therefore, this Pauline description of the human body in the First Letter to the Corinthians seems to be closely connected with the recommendations of the First Letter to the Thessalonians: "that each one of you know how to control his own body in holiness and honor" (1 Thes. 4:4). This is an important thread, perhaps the essential one, of the Pauline doctrine on purity.

St. Paul's Description of the Body and Teaching on Purity

General audience of February 4, 1981.

1. In our considerations last Wednesday on purity according to the teaching of St. Paul, we called attention to the text of the First Letter to the Corinthians. In it the Apostle presents the Church as the Body of Christ, and that offers him the opportunity to make the following reasoning about the human body: "...God arranged the organs in the body, each one of them, as he chose.... On the contrary, the parts of the body which seem to be weaker are indispensable, and those parts of the body which we think less honorable we invest with the greater honor, and our unpresentable parts are treated with greater modesty, which our more presentable parts do not require. But God has so composed the body, giving the greater honor to the inferior part, that there may be no discord in the body, but that the members may have the same care for one another" (1 Cor. 12:18, 22-25).

MAN "IS" THAT BODY

2. The Pauline "description" of the human body corresponds to the reality which consti-

tutes it: so it is a "realistic" description. At the same time, a very fine thread of evaluation is intermingled with the realism of this description, conferring on it a deeply evangelical, Christian value. Certainly, it is possible to "describe" the human body, to express its truth with the objectivity characteristic of the natural sciences; but such a description—with all its precision—cannot be adequate (that is, commensurable with its object), since it is not just a question of the body (intended as an organism, in the "somatic" sense) but of man, who expresses himself through that body and in this sense "is," I would say, that body. And so that thread of evaluation, seeing that it is a question of man as a person, is indispensable in describing the human body. Furthermore, it is necessary to say how right this evaluation is. This is one of the tasks and one of the perennial themes of the whole of culture: of literature, sculpture, painting, and also of dancing, of theatrical works, and finally of the culture of everyday life, private or social. A subject that would be worth dealing with separately.

NOT "SCIENTIFIC"

3. The Pauline description in the First Letter to the Corinthians 12:18-25 certainly does not have a "scientific" meaning: it does not present a biological study on the human organism or on human "somatics"; from this point of view it is a simple "pre-scientific" description,

moreover a concise one, made up of barely a few sentences. It has all the characteristics of common realism and is, unquestionably, sufficiently "realistic." However, what determines its specific character, what particularly justifies its presence in Holy Scripture, is precisely that evaluation intermingled with the description expressed in its "narrative-realistic" tissue. It can be said with certainty that this description would not be possible without the whole truth of creation and also without the whole truth of the "redemption of the body," which Paul professes and proclaims. It can also be affirmed that the Pauline description of the body corresponds precisely to the spiritual attitude of "respect" for the human body, due because of the "holiness" (cf. 1 Thes. 4:3-5, 7-8) which springs from the mysteries of creation and redemption. The Pauline description is equally far from Manichaean contempt for the body and from the various manifestations of a naturalistic "cult of the body."

ECHO OF INNOCENCE

4. The author of the First Letter to the Corinthians 12:18-25 has before his eyes the human body in all its truth, and so the body permeated in the first place (if it can be expressed in this way) by the whole reality of the person and of his dignity. It is, at the same time, the body of "historical" man, male and female, that is, of that man who, after sin, was con-

ceived, so to speak, within and by the reality of the man who had had the experience of original innocence. In Paul's expressions about the "unpresentable parts" of the human body, as also about the ones "which seem to be weaker" or the ones "which we think less honorable," we seem to find again the testimony of the same shame that the first human beings, male and female, had experienced after original sin. This shame was imprinted on them and on all the generations of "historical" man as the fruit of the three forms of lust (with particular reference to the lust of the flesh). And at the same time there is imprinted on this shame—as has already been highlighted in the preceding analyses—a certain "echo" of man's original innocence itself: a "negative," as it were, of the image, whose "positive" had been precisely original innocence.

RESPECT SPRINGS FROM SHAME

5. The Pauline "description" of the human body seems to confirm perfectly our previous analyses. There are, in the human body, "unpresentable parts," not because of their "somatic" nature (since a scientific and physiological description deals with all the parts and organs of the human body in a "neutral" way, with the same objectivity), but only and exclusively because there exists in man himself that shame which perceives some parts of the body as "unpresentable" and causes them to be considered such. The same shame seems, at the

same time, to be at the basis of what the Apostle writes in the First Letter to the Corinthians: "Those parts of the body which we think less honorable we invest with the greater honor, and our unpresentable parts are treated with greater modesty" (1 Cor. 12:23). Hence it can be said, therefore, that from shame there springs precisely "respect" for one's own body: respect which Paul, in the First Letter to the Thessalonians (4:4), urges us to keep. Precisely this control of the body "in holiness and honor" is considered essential for the virtue of purity.

INTERIOR HARMONY

6. Returning again to the Pauline "description" of the body, in the First Letter to the Corinthians 12:18-25, we wish to draw attention to the fact that, according to the author of the Letter, that particular effort which aims at respecting the human body and especially its "weaker" or "unpresentable" parts, corresponds to the Creator's original plan, that is, to that vision of which the Book of Genesis speaks: "God saw everything that he had made, and behold, it was very good" (Gn. 1:31). Paul writes: "God has so composed the body, giving the greater honor to the inferior parts, that there may be no discord in the body, but that the members may have the same care for one another" (1 Cor. 12:24-25). "Discord in the body," the result of which is that some parts are considered "weaker," "less honorable," and so

"unpresentable," is a further expression of the vision of man's interior state after original sin, that is, of "historical" man. The man of original innocence, male and female, of whom we read in Genesis 2:25, that they "were naked, and were not ashamed," did not even feel that "discord in the body." To the objective harmony, with which the Creator endowed the body and which Paul specifies as mutual care of the members for one another (cf. 1 Cor. 12:25), there corresponded a similar harmony within man: the harmony of the "heart." This harmony, that is precisely "purity of heart," enabled man and woman in the state of original innocence to experience simply (and in a way that originally made them both happy) the uniting power of their bodies, which was, so to speak, the "unsuspected" substratum of their personal union or *communio personarum*.

IN HOLINESS AND HONOR

7. As can be seen, in the First Letter to the Corinthians (12:18-25), the Apostle links his description of the human body with the state of "historical" man. At the threshold of this man's history there is the experience of shame connected with "discord in the body," with the sense of modesty regarding that body (and particularly those parts of it that somatically determine masculinity and femininity). However, in the same "description," Paul indicates also the way which (precisely on the basis of the

sense of shame) leads to the transformation of this state to the point of gradual victory over that "discord in the body," a victory which can and must take place in man's heart. This is precisely the way to purity, that is, "to control one's own body in holiness and honor." Paul connects the First Letter to the Corinthians (12:18-25) with the "honor" with which the First Letter to the Thessalonians (4:3-5) deals, using some equivalent expressions, when he speaks of "honor," that is, esteem, for the "less honorable," "weaker" parts of the body, and when he recommends greater "modesty" with regard to what is considered "unpresentable" in man. These expressions characterize more precisely that "honor," especially in the sphere of human relations and behavior with regard to the body; which is important both as regards one's "own" body, and of course also in mutual relations (especially between man and woman, although not limited to them).

We have no doubt that the "description" of the human body in the First Letter to the Corinthians has a fundamental meaning for the Pauline doctrine on purity as a whole.

The Virtue of Purity Is the Expression and Fruit of Life According to the Spirit

General audience of February 11, 1981.

1. During our recent Wednesday meetings we have analyzed two passages taken from the First Letter to the Thessalonians (4:3-5) and from the First Letter to the Corinthians (12:18-25), with a view to showing what seems to be essential in St. Paul's doctrine on purity, understood in the moral sense, that is, as a virtue. If in the afore-mentioned text of the First Letter to the Thessalonians we can see that purity consists in temperance, in this text, however, as also in the First Letter to the Corinthians, the element of "respect" is also highlighted. By means of such respect due to the human body (and let us add that, according to the First Letter to the Corinthians, respect is seen precisely in relation to its element of modesty), purity, as a Christian virtue, is revealed in the Pauline Letters as an effective way to become detached from what, in the human heart, is the fruit of the lust of the flesh.

Abstention "from unchastity," which implies controlling one's body "in holiness and honor," makes it possible to deduce that, according to the Apostle's doctrine, purity is a "capacity" centered on the dignity of the body, that is, on the dignity of the person in relation to his own body, to the femininity or masculinity which is manifested in this body. Purity, understood as "capacity," is precisely the expression and fruit of life "according to the Spirit" in the full meaning of the expression, that is, as a new capacity of the human being, in which the gift of the Holy Spirit bears fruit.

These two dimensions of purity—the moral dimension, that is virtue, and the charismatic dimension, namely the gift of the Holy Spirit —are present and closely connected in Paul's message. That is emphasized particularly by the Apostle in the First Letter to the Corinthians, in which he calls the body "a temple (therefore, a dwelling and shrine) of the Holy Spirit."

YOU ARE NOT YOUR OWN

2. "Do you not know that your body is a temple of the Holy Spirit within you, which you have from God? You are not your own"—Paul says to the Corinthians (1 Cor. 6:19), after having first instructed them with great severity about the moral requirements of purity. "Shun immorality. Every other sin which a man commits is outside the body; but the immoral man sins against his own body" (ibid., 6:18). The

peculiar characteristic of the sin that the Apostle stigmatizes here lies in the fact that this sin, unlike all others, is "against the body" (while other sins are "outside the body"). In this way, therefore, we find in the Pauline terminology the motivation for the expressions: "the sins of the body" or "carnal sins." Sins which are in opposition precisely to that virtue by force of which man keeps "his body in holiness and honor" (cf. 1 Thes. 4:3-5).

PROFANATION OF THE TEMPLE

3. Such sins bring with them "profanation" of the body: they deprive the man's or woman's body of the honor due to it because of the dignity of the person. However, the Apostle goes further: according to him, sin against the body is also "profanation of the temple." In Paul's eyes, it is not only the human spirit, thanks to which man is constituted as a personal subject, that decides the dignity of the human body, but even more so the supernatural reality constituted by the indwelling and the continual presence of the Holy Spirit in man—in his soul and in his body—as fruit of the redemption carried out by Christ.

It follows that man's "body" is no longer just "his own." And not only for the reason that it is the body of the person does it deserve that respect whose manifestation in the mutual conduct of men, males and females, constitutes the virtue of purity. When the Apostle writes: "Your body is a temple of the Holy Spirit within you, which you have from God" (1 Cor. 6:19), he intends to indicate yet another source of the dignity of the body, precisely the Holy Spirit, who is also the source of the moral duty deriving from this dignity.

YOU WERE BOUGHT WITH A PRICE

4. It is the reality of redemption, which is also "redemption of the body," that constitutes this source. For Paul, this mystery of faith is a living reality, geared directly to every man. Through redemption, every man has received from God again, as it were, himself and his own body. Christ has imprinted on the human body —on the body of every man and every woman— a new dignity, since in Himself the human body has been admitted, together with the soul, to union with the Person of the Son-Word. With this new dignity, through the "redemption of the body" there arose at the same time also a new obligation, of which Paul writes concisely, but in an extremely moving way: "You were bought with a price" *(ibid.,* 6:20). The fruit of redemption is, in fact, the Holy Spirit, who dwells in man and in his body as in a temple. In this Gift, which sanctifies every man, the Christian receives himself again as a gift from God. And this new, double gift is binding. The Apostle refers to this binding dimension when he writes to believers, aware of the Gift, to convince them that one must not commit "unchas-

tity," one must not sin "against one's own body" *(ibid.,* 6:18). He writes: "The body is not meant for immorality, but for the Lord, and the Lord for the body" *(ibid.,* 6:13).

It is difficult to express more concisely what the mystery of the Incarnation brings with it for every believer. The fact that the human body becomes in Jesus Christ the body of God-Man obtains for this reason, in every man, a new supernatural elevation, which every Christian must take into account in his behavior with regard to his "own" body and, of course, with regard to the other's body: man with regard to woman and woman with regard to man. The redemption of the body involves the institution, in Christ and through Christ, of a new measure of the holiness of the body. Paul refers precisely to this "holiness" in the First Letter to the Thessalonians (4:3-5), when he writes of "controlling one's own body in holiness and honor."

ONE WITH THE LORD

5. In chapter six of the First Letter to the Corinthians, Paul specifies, on the other hand, the truth about the holiness of the body, stigmatizing "unchastity," that is, the sin against the holiness of the body, the sin of impurity, with words that are even drastic: "Do you not know that your bodies are members of Christ? Shall I therefore take the members of Christ and make them members of a prostitute? Never! Do you not know that he who joins himself to a prostitute becomes one body with her? For, as it is

written, 'The two shall become one flesh.' But
he who is united to the Lord becomes one spirit
with him" (1 Cor. 6:15-17). If purity is, according to the Pauline teaching, an aspect of "life
according to the Spirit," that means that the
mystery of the redemption of the body as part of
the mystery of Christ, started in the Incarnation
and already addressed to every man through it,
bears fruit in it.

This mystery bears fruit also in purity,
understood as a particular commitment based
on ethics. The fact that we were "bought with
a price" (1 Cor. 6:20), that is, at the price
of Christ's redemption, gives rise precisely to
a special commitment, that is, the duty of
"controlling one's body in holiness and honor."
Awareness of the redemption of the body operates in the human will in favor of abstention
from "unchastity"; in acts, in fact, for the purpose of causing man to acquire an appropriate
ability or capacity, called the virtue of purity.

What can be seen from the words of the
First Letter to the Corinthians (6:15-17) about
Paul's teaching on the Christian virtue of purity
as the implementation of life "according to the
Spirit" is of particular depth and has the power
of the supernatural realism of faith. We will
have to come back to reflection on this subject
more than once.

The Pauline Doctrine of Purity as "Life According to the Spirit"

General audience of March 18, 1981.

1. At our meeting some weeks ago, we concentrated our attention on the passage in the First Letter to the Corinthians, in which St. Paul calls the human body "a temple of the Holy Spirit." He writes: "Do you not know that your body is a temple of the Holy Spirit within you, which you have from God? You are not your own; you were bought with a price" (1 Cor. 6:19-20). "Do you not know that your bodies are members of Christ?" (1 Cor. 6:15). The Apostle points out the mystery of the "redemption of the body," carried out by Christ, as a source of a special moral duty which commits the Christian to purity, to what Paul himself defines elsewhere as the necessity of "controlling his own body in holiness and honor" (1 Thes. 4:4).

PIETY SERVES PURITY

2. However, we would not completely discover the riches of the thought contained in the Pauline texts, if we did not note that the mystery of redemption bears fruit in man also in a charismatic way. The Holy Spirit who, according to the Apostle's words, enters the

human body as His own "temple," dwells there and operates together with His spiritual gifts. Among these gifts, known in the history of spirituality as the seven gifts of the Holy Spirit (cf. Is. 11:2, according to the Septuagint and the Vulgate), the one most congenial to the virtue of purity seems to be the gift of "piety" *(eusebeia, donum pietatis)*.[1] If purity prepares man to "control his own body in holiness and honor," as we read in the First Letter to the Thessalonians (4:3-5), piety, which is a gift of the Holy Spirit, seems to serve purity in a particular way, making the human subject sensitive to that dignity which is characteristic of the human body by virtue of the mystery of creation and redemption. Thanks to the gift of piety, Paul's words: "Do you not know that your body is a temple of the Holy Spirit within you.... You are not your own" (1 Cor. 6:19), acquire the eloquence of an experience of the nuptial meaning of the body and of the freedom of the gift connected with it, in which the profound aspect of purity and its organic link with love is revealed.

FRUIT OF
THE SPIRIT'S INDWELLING

3. Although control of one's body "in holiness and honor" is acquired through abstention from "immorality"—and this way is indispensable—yet it always bears fruit in deeper experience of that love, which was inscribed "from the beginning," according to the image and likeness of God Himself, in the whole human being

and therefore also in his body. Therefore, Saint Paul ends his argumentation in the First Letter to the Corinthians, chapter six, with a significant exhortation: "So glorify God in your body" (v. 20). Purity, as the virtue, that is, the capacity of "controlling one's body in holiness and honor," together with the gift of piety, as the fruit of the dwelling of the Holy Spirit in the "temple" of the body, brings about in the body such a fullness of dignity in interpersonal relations that God Himself is thereby glorified. Purity is the glory of the human body before God. It is God's glory in the human body, through which masculinity and femininity are manifested. From purity springs that extraordinary beauty which permeates every sphere of men's mutual common life and makes it possible to express in it simplicity and depth, cordiality and the unrepeatable authenticity of personal trust. (There will perhaps be another opportunity later to deal with this subject more fully. The connection of purity with love and also the connection of purity in love with that gift of the Holy Spirit, piety, is a part of the theology of the body which is little known, but which deserves particular study. That will be possible in the course of the analysis concerning the sacramentality of marriage.)

IN THE OLD TESTAMENT

4. And now a brief reference to the Old Testament. The Pauline doctrine about purity, understood as "life according to the Spirit,"

seems to indicate a certain continuity with regard to the Wisdom Books of the Old Testament. We find there, for example, the following prayer to obtain purity in thought, word and deed: "O Lord, Father and God of my life... remove from me evil desire, let neither gluttony nor lust overcome me" (Sir. 23:4-6). Purity is, in fact, the condition for finding wisdom and following it, as we read in the same Book: "I directed my soul to her (that is, to Wisdom), and through purification I found her" (Sir. 51:20). We could also take into consideration in a way the text of the Book of Wisdom (8:21), known by the liturgy in the Vulgate version: *"Scivi quoniam aliter non possum esse continens, nisi Deus det; et hoc ipsum erat sapientiae, scire, cuius esset hoc donum."*[2]

According to this concept, it is not so much purity that is a condition for wisdom, but wisdom that is a condition for purity, as for a special gift of God. It seems that already in the above-mentioned Wisdom texts the double meaning of purity takes shape: as a virtue and as a gift. The virtue is in the service of wisdom, and wisdom is a preparation to receive the gift that comes from God. This gift strengthens the virtue and makes it possible to enjoy, in wisdom, the fruits of a behavior and life that are pure.

THE SIGHT OF GOD

5. Just as Christ, in His beatitude in the Sermon on the Mount which refers to the "pure in heart," highlights the "sight of God," the

fruit of purity, and in an eschatological perspective, so Paul in his turn sheds light on its diffusion in the dimensions of temporality, when he writes: "To the pure all things are pure, but to the corrupt and unbelieving nothing is pure; their very minds and consciences are corrupted. They profess to know God, but they deny him by their deeds..." (Ti. 1:15f.). These words can also refer both to the general and to the specific meaning of purity, as to the characteristic note of all moral good. For the Pauline concept of purity, in the sense spoken of in the First Letter to the Thessalonians (4:3-5) and the First Letter to the Corinthians (6:13-20), that is, in the sense of "life according to the Spirit," the anthropology of rebirth in the Holy Spirit (cf. also Jn. 3:5ff.) seems to be fundamental—as can be seen from these considerations of ours as a whole. It grows from roots set in the reality of the redemption of the body, carried out by Christ: redemption, whose ultimate expression is the resurrection. There are profound reasons for connecting the whole theme of purity with the words of the Gospel, in which Christ refers to the resurrection (and that will be the subject of the further stage of our considerations). Here we have mainly linked it with the ethos of the redemption of the body.

APPEAL TO THE HEART

6. The way of understanding and presenting purity—inherited from the tradition of the Old Testament and characteristic of the

Wisdom Books—was certainly an indirect, but nonetheless real, preparation for the Pauline doctrine about purity understood as "life according to the Spirit." That way unquestionably helped many listeners of the Sermon on the Mount to understand Christ's words, when, explaining the commandment, "You shall not commit adultery," He appealed to the human "heart." In this way our reflections as a whole have been able to show, at least to a certain extent, how rich and profound the doctrine on purity is in its biblical and evangelical sources themselves.

FOOTNOTES

1. In the Greco-Roman period *eusebeia* or *pietas* generally referred to the veneration of the gods (as "devotion"), but it still kept its broader original meaning of respect for vital structures.

Eusebeia defined the mutual behavior of relatives, relations between husband and wife, and also the attitude due by the legions towards Caesar or by slaves to their masters.

In the New Testament, only the later writings apply *eusebeia* to Christians; in the older writings this term characterizes "good pagans" (Acts 10:2, 7; 17:23).

And so the Greek *eusebeia*, as also the *donum pietatis*, while they certainly refer to divine veneration, have a wide basis in the connotation of interpersonal relations (cf. W. Foerster, art. *eusebeia*, in: "Theological Dictionary of the New Testament," ed. G. Kittel-G. Bromiley, vol. VII, Grand Rapids 1971, Eerdmans, pp. 177-182).

2. This version of the Vulgate, retained by the Neo-Vulgate and by the liturgy, quoted several times by Augustine *(De S. Virg.,* par. 43; *Confess.* VI, 11; X, 29; *Serm.* CLX, 7), changes, however, the meaning of the original Greek, which can be translated as follows: "Knowing that I would not have obtained it [Wisdom] otherwise, if God had not granted it to me...."

Positive Function
of Purity of Heart

General audience of April 1, 1981.

1. Before concluding the series of considerations concerning the words uttered by Jesus
Christ in the Sermon on the Mount, it is
necessary to recall these words once more and
briefly retrace the thread of ideas whose basis
they constitute. Here is the tenor of Jesus'
words: "You have heard that it was said, 'You
shall not commit adultery.' But I say to you that
everyone who looks at a woman lustfully has
already committed adultery with her in his
heart" (Mt. 5:27-28). They are concise words,
which call for deep reflection, in the same way
as the words in which Christ referred to the
"beginning." To the Pharisees who—referring
to the law of Moses which admitted the so-called
act of repudiation—had asked Him: "Is it lawful
to divorce one's wife for any cause?" He replied:
"Have you not read that he who made them
from the beginning made them male and
female?... For this reason a man shall leave his
father and mother and be joined to his wife, and
the two shall become one flesh.... What therefore God has joined together, let not man put

asunder" (Mt. 19:3-6). These words, too, called for a deep reflection, to derive all the riches contained in them. A reflection of this kind enabled us to outline the true theology of the body.

TRUTH ROOTED IN
MAN'S ORIGINAL INNOCENCE

2. Following the reference made by Christ to the "beginning," we dedicated a series of reflections to the relative texts in the Book of Genesis, which deal precisely with that "beginning." There emerged from the analysis made not only an image of the situation of man—male and female—in the state of original innocence, but also the theological basis of the truth about man and about his particular vocation which springs from the eternal mystery of the person: the image of God, incarnate in the visible and corporeal fact of the masculinity or femininity of the human person. This truth is at the basis of the answer given by Christ with regard to the nature of marriage, and in particular its indissolubility. It is truth about man, truth rooted in the state of original innocence, truth which must therefore be understood in the context of that situation prior to sin, as we tried to do in the preceding series of our reflections.

3. At the same time, however, it is necessary to consider, understand and interpret the same fundamental truth about man, his being male and female, in the prism of another situation: that is, of the one that was formed through

the breaking of the first covenant with the Creator, that is, through original sin. Such truth about man—male and female—should be seen in the context of his hereditary sinfulness. And it is precisely here that we find Christ's enunciation in the Sermon on the Mount. It is obvious that in the Scriptures of the Old and New Covenant there are many narratives, phrases and words which confirm the same truth, that is, that "historical" man bears within him the inheritance of original sin; nevertheless, Christ's words spoken in the Sermon on the Mount seem to have—with all their concise enunciation—a particularly rich eloquence. This is shown also by the analyses made previously, which gradually revealed what those words contain. To clarify the statements concerning lust, it is necessary to grasp the biblical meaning of lust itself—of the three forms of lust—and principally that of the flesh. Then, little by little, we arrive at understanding why Jesus defines that lust (precisely: "looking at lustfully") as "adultery committed in the heart." Making the relative analyses, we tried, at the same time, to understand what meaning Christ's words had for His immediate listeners, brought up in the tradition of the Old Testament, that is, in the tradition of the legislative texts, as well as the prophetic and "sapiential" ones; and furthermore, what meaning Christ's words can have for the man of every other era, and in particular for modern man, considering his various cultural conditionings. We are convinced, in fact, that these words, in their essential content, refer to the man of every time and every place. Their comprehensive value consists also in this: they proclaim to each one the truth that is valid and substantial for him.

AN ETHICAL TRUTH

4. What is this truth? Unquestionably, it is a truth of an ethical nature and therefore, in a word, a truth of a normative nature, just as the truth contained in the commandment: "You shall not commit adultery," is normative. The interpretation of this commandment, made by Christ, indicates the evil that must be avoided and overcome—precisely the evil of lust of the flesh—and at the same time points out the good for which the way is opened by the overcoming of desire. This good is "purity of heart," of which Christ speaks in the same context of the Sermon on the Mount. From the biblical point of view, "purity of heart" means freedom from every kind of sin or guilt, and not just from sins that concern the "lust of the flesh." However, we are dealing here particularly with one of the aspects of that "purity," which constitutes the opposite of adultery "committed in the heart." If that "purity of heart," about which we are concerned, is understood according to Saint Paul's thought as "life according to the Spirit," then the Pauline context offers us a complete image of the content present in the words spoken by Christ in the Sermon on the Mount.

They contain a truth of an ethical nature; they warn us against evil and indicate the moral good of human conduct. In fact, they direct listeners to avoid the evil of lust and acquire purity of heart. These words therefore have a meaning that is both normative and indicative. Directing towards the good of "purity of heart," they indicate, at the same time, the values towards which the human heart can and must aspire.

CHRIST'S WORDS REALISTIC

5. Hence the question: what truth, valid for every man, is contained in Christ's words? We must answer that not only an ethical truth, but also the essential truth, the anthropological truth, about man is contained in them. It is precisely for this reason that we go back to these words in formulating here the theology of the body, closely related to and, so to speak, in the perspective of the preceding words in which Christ had referred to "the beginning." It can be affirmed that, with their expressive evangelical eloquence, the man of original innocence is, in a way, recalled to the consciousness of the man of lust.

But Christ's words are realistic. They do not try to make the human heart return to the state of original innocence, which man left behind him at the moment when he committed original sin; on the contrary, they indicate to him the way to a purity of heart which is possible and accessible to him even in the state of hereditary sinfulness. This is the purity of the "man of lust," who is inspired, however, by the word of the Gospel and open to "life according to the Spirit" (in conformity with St. Paul's words), that is, the purity of the man of lust who is entirely enveloped by the "redemption of the body" carried out by Christ. Precisely for this reason we find in the words of the Sermon on the Mount the reference to the "heart," that is, to interior man. Interior man must open himself to life according to the Spirit, in order to participate in evangelical purity of heart: in order to rediscover and realize the value of the body, freed through redemption from the bonds of lust.

The normative meaning of Christ's words is deeply rooted in their anthropological meaning, in the dimension of human interiority.

FELT WITH THE HEART

6. According to the evangelical doctrine, developed in such a stupendous way in Paul's letters, purity is not just abstention from unchastity (cf. 1 Thes. 4:3), or temperance, but it also, at the same time, opens the way to a more and more perfect discovery of the dignity of the human body, that body which is organically connected with the freedom of the gift of the person in the complete authenticity of his personal subjectivity, male or female. In this way purity, in the sense of temperance,

matures in the heart of the man who cultivates it and tends to reveal and strengthen the nuptial meaning of the body in its integral truth. Precisely this truth must be known interiorly; it must, in a way, be "felt with the heart," in order that the mutual relations of man and of woman —even mere looks—may reacquire that authentically nuptial content of their meanings. And it is precisely this content which is indicated by "purity of heart" in the Gospel.

ENJOYING THE VICTORY

7. If in the interior experience of man (that is, the man of lust), "temperance" takes shape, so to speak, as a negative function, the analysis of Christ's words spoken in the Sermon on the Mount and connected with the texts of St. Paul enables us to shift this meaning towards the positive function of purity of heart. In mature purity man enjoys the fruits of the victory won over lust, a victory of which St. Paul writes, exhorting man to "control his own body in holiness and honor" (1 Thes. 4:4). Precisely in such mature purity, in fact, the efficacy of the gift of the Holy Spirit, whose "temple" the human body is (cf. 1 Cor. 6:19), is partly manifested. This gift is above all that of piety *(donum pietatis)*, which restores to the experience of the body—especially when it is a question of the sphere of the mutual relations of man and woman—all its simplicity, its explicitness and also its interior joy. This is, as can be seen, a spiritual climate which is very different from

the "passion of lust" of which Paul writes (and which we know, moreover, from the preceding analyses; just remember Sirach 26:13, 15-18). The satisfaction of the passions is, in fact, one thing, and the joy that man finds in mastering himself more fully is another thing, since in this way he can also become more fully a real gift for another person.

The words spoken by Christ in the Sermon on the Mount direct the human heart precisely towards this joy. We must entrust ourselves, our thoughts and our actions, to them, in order to find joy and give it to others.

Pronouncements of the Magisterium Apply Christ's Words Today

General audience of April 8, 1981.

1. The time has now come to conclude the reflections and analyses based on the words uttered by Christ in the Sermon on the Mount, with which He appealed to the human heart, exhorting it to purity: "You have heard that it was said, You shall not commit adultery. But I say to you that everyone who looks at a woman lustfully has already committed adultery with her in his heart" (Mt. 5:27-28). We have said several times that these words, spoken once to the limited number of listeners to that Sermon, refer to man of all times and places, and appeal to the human heart, in which there is inscribed the most interior and, in a way, the most essential design of history. It is the history of good and evil (whose beginning is connected, in the Book of Genesis, with the mysterious tree of the knowledge of good and evil) and, at the same time, it is the history of salvation, whose word is the Gospel, and whose power is the Holy Spirit, given to those who accept the Gospel with a sincere heart.

CHRIST'S WORDS TEACH

2. If Christ's appeal to the human "heart" and, still earlier, His reference to the "beginning," enables us to construct or at least to outline an anthropology, which we can call "theology of the body," such theology is, at the same time, pedagogy. Pedagogy aims at educating man, setting before him the requirements, motivating them, and pointing out the ways that lead to their fulfillment. Christ's pronouncements have also this purpose: they are "pedagogical" enunciations. They contain a pedagogy of the body, expressed in a concise and at the same time extremely complete way. Both the answer given to the Pharisees with regard to the indissolubility of marriage, and the words of the Sermon on the Mount concerning the mastery of lust, prove—at least indirectly—that the Creator has assigned as a task to man his body, his masculinity and femininity; and that in masculinity and femininity He, in a way, assigned to him as a task his humanity, the dignity of the person, and also the clear sign of the interpersonal "communion" in which man fulfills himself through the authentic gift of himself. Setting before man the requirements conforming to the tasks entrusted to him, at the same time the Creator points out to man, male and female, the ways that lead to assuming and discharging them.

SELF-EDUCATION OF MAN

3. Analyzing these key texts of the Bible to their very roots, we discover precisely that

anthropology which can be called "theology of the body." And it is this theology of the body which is the basis of the most suitable method of the pedagogy of the body, that is, the education (in fact the self-education) of man. That takes on particular relevance for modern man, whose science in the field of biophysiology and biomedicine has made great progress. However, this science deals with man under a determined "aspect" and so is partial rather than global. We know well the functions of the body as an organism, the functions connected with the masculinity and femininity of the human person. But this science, in itself, does not yet develop the awareness of the body as a sign of the person, as a manifestation of the spirit.

The whole development of modern science, regarding the body as an organism, has rather the character of biological knowledge, because it is based on the separation, in man, of that which is corporeal in him from that which is spiritual. Using such a one-sided knowledge of the functions of the body as an organism, it is not difficult to arrive at treating the body, in a more or less systematic way, as an object of manipulations. In this case man ceases, so to speak, to identify himself subjectively with his own body, because it is deprived of the meaning and the dignity deriving from the fact that this body is proper to the person. We here touch upon problems often demanding fundamental solutions, which are impossible without an integral view of man.

NEED OF ADEQUATE
SPIRITUAL MATURITY

4. Precisely here it appears clear that the theology of the body, which we derive from those key texts of Christ's words, becomes the fundamental method of pedagogy, that is, of man's education from the point of view of the body, in full consideration of his masculinity and femininity. That pedagogy can be understood under the aspect of a specific "spirituality of the body." The body, in fact, in its masculinity or femininity is given as a task to the human spirit (this was expressed in a stupendous way by St. Paul in his own characteristic language), and by means of an adequate maturity of the spirit it too becomes a sign of the person, of which the person is conscious, and authentic "matter" in the communion of the persons. In other words: man, through his spiritual maturity, discovers the nuptial meaning proper to the body.

Christ's words in the Sermon on the Mount indicate that lust in itself does not reveal that meaning to man, but on the contrary dims and obscures it. Purely "biological" knowledge of the functions of the body as an organism, connected with the masculinity and femininity of the human person, is capable of helping to discover the true nuptial meaning of the body, only if it is accompanied by an adequate spiritual maturity of the human person. Otherwise, such knowledge can have quite the opposite effect; and this is confirmed by many experiences of our time.

5. From this point of view it is necessary to consider prudently the pronouncements of the modern Church. Their adequate understanding and interpretation, as well as their practical application (that is, precisely, pedagogy) demands that deep theology of the body which, in a word, we derive mainly from the key words of Christ. As for the pronouncements of the Church in modern times, it is necessary to study the chapter entitled, "The dignity of marriage and the family," of the Pastoral Constitution of the Second Vatican Council *(Gaudium et spes,* part II, chap. I) and, subsequently, Paul VI's Encyclical *Humanae vitae.* Without any doubt, the words of Christ, which we have analyzed at great length, had no other purpose than to emphasize the dignity of marriage and the family; hence the fundamental convergence between them and the content of both the above-mentioned statements of the modern Church. Christ was speaking to the man of all times and places; the pronouncements of the Church aim at applying Christ's words to the here and now, and therefore they must be reread according to the key of that theology and that pedagogy which find roots and support in Christ's words.

It is difficult here to make a total analysis of the cited pronouncements of the supreme

Magisterium of the Church. We will confine ourselves to quoting some passages. Here is how the Second Vatican Council—placing among the most urgent problems of the Church in the modern world "the dignity of marriage and the family"—characterizes the situation that exists in this area: "The happy picture of the dignity of these partnerships (that is, marriage and family) is not reflected everywhere, but is overshadowed by polygamy, the plague of divorce, so-called free love, and similar blemishes; furthermore, married love is too often dishonored by selfishness, hedonism, and unlawful contraceptive practices" (*Gaudium et spes*, no. 47). Paul VI, setting forth this last problem in the Encyclical *Humanae vitae*, writes among other things: "Another thing that gives cause for alarm is that a man who grows accustomed to the use of contraceptive methods may forget the reverence due to a woman, and, disregarding her physical and emotional equilibrium, reduce her to being a mere instrument for the satisfaction of his own desires, no longer considering her as his partner whom he should surround with care and affection" *(Humanae vitae, no. 17).*

Are we not here in the sphere of the same concern which once dictated Christ's words on the unity and indissolubility of marriage, as well as those of the Sermon on the Mount, concerning purity of heart and mastery of the lust of the flesh, words that were later developed with so much acuteness by the Apostle Paul?

DEMANDS OF CHRISTIAN MORALITY

6. In the same spirit the author of the Encyclical *Humanae vitae*, speaking of the demands of Christian morality, presents at the same time the possibility of fulfilling them when he writes: "The mastery of instinct by one's reason and free will undoubtedly demands an asceticism"—Paul VI uses this term—"so that the affective manifestations of conjugal life may be in keeping with right order, in particular with regard to the observance of periodic continence. Yet this discipline which is proper to the purity of married couples, far from harming conjugal love, rather confers on it a higher human value. It demands a continual effort (precisely this effort was called above "asceticism"), yet, thanks to its beneficent influence, husband and wife fully develop their personalities, enrich each other with spiritual values.... It favors attention for one's partner, helps both parties to drive out selfishness, the enemy of true love, and deepens their sense of responsibility...." *(Humanae vitae, no. 21).*

NEED OF MAGISTERIAL PRONOUNCEMENTS

7. Let us pause on these few passages. They—particularly the last one—clearly show how indispensable, for an adequate understanding of the pronouncement of the Magisterium of the modern Church, is that theology

of the body, whose foundations we sought especially in the words of Christ Himself. It is precisely that theology—as we have already said—that becomes the fundamental method of the whole Christian pedagogy of the body. Referring to the words quoted, it can be affirmed that the purpose of the pedagogy of the body lies precisely in ensuring that the "affective manifestations"—particularly those "proper to conjugal life"—be in conformity with the moral order, or, in a word, with the dignity of the persons. In these words there returns the problem of the mutual relationship between "eros" and "ethos," with which we have already dealt. Theology, understood as a method of the pedagogy of the body, prepares us also for further reflections on the sacramentality of human life and, in particular, of married life.

The Gospel of purity of heart, yesterday and today: concluding with this phrase this cycle of our considerations—before going on to the next one, in which the basis of analyses will be Christ's words on the resurrection of the body—we still wish to devote some attention to "the need of creating an atmosphere favorable to education in chastity," with which Paul VI's encyclical deals (cf. *Humanae vitae*, no. 22), and we wish to focus these observations on the problem of the ethos of the body in works of artistic culture, with particular reference to the situations we encounter in modern life.

The Human Body, Subject of Works of Art

General audience of April 15, 1981.

Today's audience falls in the course of Holy Week, the "great" week of the liturgical year, because it makes us relive very closely the Paschal Mystery, in which "the revelation of God's merciful love reaches its climax" (cf. *Dives in misericordia*, no. 8).

While I call on each of you to take part fervently in the liturgical celebrations of these days, I form the hope that everyone will recognize with exultation and gratitude the unique gift of having been saved by the passion and death of Christ. The whole history of humanity is illuminated and guided by this incomparable event: God, infinite goodness, poured it out with inexpressible love by means of Christ's supreme sacrifice. So while we prepare to raise our hymn of glory to Christ, the Conqueror of death, we must eliminate from our souls everything that may be in contrast with a meeting with Him. To see Him through faith, it is necessary, in fact, to be purified by the sacrament of forgiveness and sustained by the persevering commitment of a deep renewal of the spirit and of that interior conversion which is the start in ourselves of the "new creation" (2 Cor. 5:17), of which the risen Christ is the first fruits and the certain pledge.

Then Easter will represent for each of us a meeting with Christ.

It is what I earnestly wish for everyone.

CONTROL OF THE BODY "IN HOLINESS AND HONOR"

1. In our preceding reflections—both in the analysis of Christ's words, in which He refers to the "beginning," and during the Sermon on the Mount, that is, when He refers to the human "heart"—we have tried, systematically, to show how the dimension of man's personal subjectivity is an indispensable element present in theological hermeneutics, which we must discover and presuppose at the basis of the problem of the human body. Therefore, not only the objective reality of the body, but far more, as it seems, subjective consciousness and also the subjective "experience" of the body, enter at every step into the structure of the biblical texts, and therefore require to be taken into consideration and find their reflection in theology. Consequently theological hermeneutics must always take these two aspects into account. We cannot consider the body an objective reality outside the personal subjectivity of man, of human beings: male and female. Nearly all the problems of the "ethos of the body" are

bound up at the same time with its ontological identification as the body of the person, and with the content and quality of the subjective experience, that is, of the "life" both of one's own body and in its interhuman relations, and in particular in the perennial "man-woman" relationship. Also the words of the First Letter to the Thessalonians, in which the author exhorts us to "control our own body in holiness and honor" (that is, the whole problem of "purity of heart") indicate, without any doubt, these two dimensions.

DIMENSIONS CONCERNING ATTITUDES OF PERSONS

2. They are dimensions which directly concern concrete, living men, their attitudes and behavior. Works of culture, especially of art, enable those dimensions of "being a body" and "experiencing the body" to extend, in a way, outside these living men. Man meets the "reality of the body" and "experiences the body" even when it becomes a subject of creative activity, a work of art, a content of culture. Although, generally speaking, it must be recognized that this contact takes place on the plane of aesthetic experience, in which it is a question of viewing the work of art (in Greek *aisthá nomai:* I look, I observe)—and therefore that, in the given case, it is a question of the objectivized body, outside its ontological identity, in a different way and according to the

criteria characteristic of artistic activity—yet the man who is admitted to viewing in this way is *a priori* too deeply bound up with the meaning of the prototype, or model, which in this case is himself—the living man and the living human body—to be able to detach and separate completely that act, substantially an aesthetic one, of the work in itself and of its contemplation from those dynamisms or reactions of behavior and from the evaluations which direct that first experience and that first way of living. This looking, which is, by its very nature, "aesthetic," cannot be completely isolated, in man's subjective conscience, from that "looking" of which Christ speaks in the Sermon on the Mount: warning against lust.

CREATING A CLIMATE
FAVORABLE TO PURITY

3. In this way, therefore, the whole sphere of aesthetic experiences is, at the same time, in the area of the ethos of the body. Rightly, therefore, we must think here too of the necessity of creating a climate favorable to purity; this climate can, in fact, be threatened not only in the very way in which the relations and society of living men take place, but also in the area of the objectivizations characteristic of works of culture; in the area of social communications: when it is a question of the spoken or written word; in the area of the image, that is, of representation and vision, both in the traditional

meaning of this term and in the modern one. In this way we reach the various fields and products of artistic, plastic and dramatic culture, as also that based on modern audio-visual techniques. In this field, a vast and very differentiated one, we must ask ourselves a question in the light of the ethos of the body, outlined in the analyses made so far on the human body as an object of culture.

LIVING HUMAN BODY CREATES OBJECT OF ART

4. First of all it must be noted that the human body is a perennial object of culture, in the widest meaning of the term, for the simple reason that man himself is a subject of culture, and in his cultural and creative activity he involves his humanity, including also his body. In these reflections, however, we must restrict the concept of "object of culture," limiting ourselves to the concept understood as the "subject" of works of culture and in particular of works of art. It is a question, in a word, of the thematic nature, that is, of the "objectivation" of the body in these works. Some distinctions must, however, be made here at once, even if by way of example. One thing is the living human body, of man and of woman, which creates in itself the object of art and the work of art (such as, for example, in the theater, in the ballet and, up to a certain point, also in the course of a concert); and another thing is the body as the

model of the work of art, as in the plastic arts, sculpture or painting. Is it possible to put also films or the photographic art in a wide sense on the same level? It seems so, although, from the point of view of the body as object-theme, a quite essential difference takes place in this case. In painting or sculpture the man-body always remains a model, undergoing specific elaboration on the part of the artist. In the film, and even more in the photographic art, it is not the model that is transfigured, but the living man is reproduced: and in this case man, the human body, is not a model for the work of art, but the object of a reproduction obtained by means of suitable techniques.

AN IMPORTANT DISTINCTION

5. It should be pointed out straightaway that the above-mentioned distinction is important from the point of view of the ethos of the body in works of culture. And it should be added at once that artistic reproduction, when it becomes the content of representation and transmission (on television or in films), loses, in a way, its fundamental contact with the man-body, of which it is a reproduction, and very often becomes an "anonymous" object, just like, for example, an anonymous photographic document published in illustrated magazines, or an image diffused on the screens of the whole world. This anonymity is the effect of the "propagation" of the image-reproduction of the

human body, objectivized first with the help of the techniques of reproduction, which—as has been recalled above—seem to be essentially differentiated from the transfiguration of the model typical of the work of art, especially in the plastic arts. Well, this anonymity (which, moreover, is a way of "veiling" or "hiding" the identity of the person reproduced) also constitutes a specific problem from the point of view of the ethos of the human body in works of culture and particularly in the modern works of mass culture, as it is called.

Let us confine ourselves today to these preliminary considerations, which have a fundamental meaning for the ethos of the human body in works of artistic culture. Subsequently these considerations will make us aware of how closely bound they are to the words which Christ spoke in the Sermon on the Mount, comparing "looking lustfully" with "adultery committed in the heart." The extension of these words to the area of artistic culture is of particular importance, insofar as it is a question of "creating an atmosphere favorable to chastity," of which Paul VI speaks in his Encyclical *Humanae vitae*. Let us try to understand this subject in a very deep and fundamental way.

Reflections on
the Ethos of the Human Body
in Works of Artistic Culture

General audience of April 22, 1981.

Dear brothers and sisters,

Paschal joy is still alive and present within us during this solemn octave, and the liturgy makes us repeat fervently: "The Lord has risen, as he had foretold; let us all rejoice and exult, because he reigns for ever, alleluia."

So let us prepare our hearts for grace and joy; let us raise our sacrifice of praise to the Paschal Victim, because the Lamb has redeemed His flock and the Innocent One has reconciled us sinners with the Father.

Christ, our Pasch, has risen and we have risen with Him, so that we must seek the things of heaven, where Christ sits at the right hand of God, and we must also enjoy the things that are above, according to the invitation of the Apostle Paul (cf. Col. 3:1-2).

While God makes us pass, in Christ, from death to life, from darkness to light, preparing us for heavenly goods, we must aim at goals of luminous works, in justice and in truth. The way we have to traverse is a long one, but God strengthens and sustains our unshakable hope of victory: may meditation on the Paschal Mystery accompany us in a particular way in these days.

A PROBLEM
WITH VERY DEEP ROOTS

1. Let us now reflect—with regard to Christ's words uttered in the Sermon on the Mount—on the problem of the ethos of the human body in works of artistic culture. This problem has very deep roots. It is opportune to recall here the series of analyses carried out in connection with Christ's reference to the "beginning," and subsequently to the reference He made to the human "heart," in the Sermon on the Mount. The human body—the naked human body in the whole truth of its masculinity and femininity—has the meaning of a gift of the person to the person. The ethos of the body, that is, the ethical norms that govern its nakedness, because of the dignity of the personal subject, is closely connected with that system of reference, understood as the nuptial system, in which the giving of one party meets the appropriate and adequate response of the other party to the gift. This response decides the reciprocity of the gift.

The artistic objectivization of the human body in its male and female nakedness, in order to make it first of all a model and then the subject of the work of art, is always to a certain extent a going outside of this original and, for the body, its specific configuration of interpersonal donation. That constitutes, in a way, an uprooting of the human body from this configuration and its transfer to the dimension of artistic objectivation: the specific dimension of the work of art or of the reproduction typical of the film and photographic techniques of our time.

In each of these dimensions—and in a different way in each one—the human body loses that deeply subjective meaning of the gift, and becomes an object destined for the knowledge of many, in such a way that those who look at, assimilate or even, in a way, take possession of what evidently exists, in fact should exist essentially at the level of a gift, made by the person to the person, not just in the image but in the living man. Actually, that "taking possession" already happens at another level—that is, at the level of the object of the transfiguration or artistic reproduction. However it is impossible not to perceive that from the point of view of the ethos of the body, deeply understood, a problem arises here. A very delicate problem, which has its levels of intensity according to various motives and circumstances both as regards artistic activity and as regards knowledge of the work of art or of its reproduction. The fact that this problem is raised does not mean that the human body, in its nakedness, cannot become a subject of works of art—but only that this problem is not purely aesthetic, nor morally indifferent.

ORIGINAL SHAME—
A PERMANENT ELEMENT

2. In our preceding analyses (especially with regard to Christ's reference to the "beginning"), we devoted a great deal of space to the meaning of shame, trying to understand the difference between the situation—and the state —of original innocence, in which "they were both naked, and were not ashamed" (Gn. 2:25), and, subsequently, between the situation—and the state—of sinfulness, in which there arose between man and woman, together with shame, the specific necessity of privacy with regard to their own bodies.

In the heart of man, subject to lust, this necessity serves, even indirectly, to ensure the gift and the possibility of mutual donation. This necessity also forms man's way of acting as "an object of culture," in the widest meaning of the term. If culture shows an explicit tendency to cover the nakedness of the human body, it certainly does so not only for climatic reasons, but also in relation to the process of growth of man's personal sensitivity. The anonymous nakedness of the man-object contrasts with the progress of the truly human culture of morals. It is probably possible to confirm this also in the life of so-called primitive populations. The process of refining personal human sensitivity is certainly a factor and fruit of culture.

Beyond the need of shame, that is, of the privacy of one's own body (on which the biblical sources give such precise information in Genesis 3), there is a deeper norm: that of the gift, directed towards the very depths of the personal subject or towards the other person —especially in the man-woman relationship according to the perennial norms regulating the mutual donation. In this way, in the processes of human culture, understood in the wide sense, we note—even in man's state of hereditary sinfulness—quite an explicit continuity of the nuptial meaning of the body in its masculinity and femininity. That original shame, known already from the first chapters of the Bible, is a permanent element of culture and morals. It belongs to the genesis of the ethos of the human body.

PERSONAL SENSITIVITY

3. The man of developed sensitivity overcomes, with difficulty and interior resistance, the limit of that shame. This is seen clearly even in situations which justify the necessity of undressing the body, such as, for example, in the case of medical examinations or operations. Mention should also be made particularly of other circumstances, such as, for example, those of concentration camps or places of extermination, where the violation of bodily shame is a method used deliberately to destroy personal sensitivity and the sense of human dignity

The same rule is confirmed everywhere —though in different ways. Following personal sensitivity, man does not wish to become an object for others through his own anonymous nakedness, nor does he wish the other to become an object for him in a similar way. Evidently "he does not wish" this to the extent to which he lets himself be guided by the sense of the dignity of the human body. There are, in fact, various motives which can induce, incite and even press man to act in a way contrary to the requirements of the dignity of the human body, a dignity connected with personal sensitivity. It cannot be forgotten that the fundamental interior "situation" of "historical" man is the state of threefold lust (cf. 1 Jn. 2:16). This state—and, in particular, the lust of the flesh—makes itself felt in various ways, both in the interior impulses of the human heart and in the whole climate of interhuman relations and social morals.

WHEN DEEP GOVERNING RULES ARE VIOLATED

4. We cannot forget this, not even when it is a question of the broad sphere of artistic culture, particularly that of visual and spectacular character, as also when it is a question of "mass" culture, so significant for our times and connected with the use of the media of audiovisual communication. A question arises: when and in what case is this sphere of man's activity—from the point of view of the ethos of the body—regarded as "pornovision," just as in

literature some writings were and are often regarded as "pornography" (this second term is an older one).

Both take place when the limit of shame, that is, of personal sensitivity with regard to what is connected with the human body, with its nakedness, is overstepped, when in the work of art or by means of the media of audiovisual reproduction the right to the privacy of the body in its masculinity or femininity, is violated —and in the last analysis—when those deep governing rules of the gift and of mutual donation, which are inscribed in this femininity and masculinity through the whole structure of the human being, are violated. This deep inscription—or rather incision—decides the nuptial meaning of the human body, that is, of the fundamental call it receives to form the "communion of persons" and take part in it.

Breaking off at this point our consideration, which we intend to continue next Wednesday, it should be noted that observance or nonobservance of these norms, so deeply connected with man's personal sensitivity, cannot be a matter of indifference for the problem of "creating a climate favorable to chastity" in life and social education.

Art Must Not Violate
the Right to Privacy

General audience of April 29, 1981.

Dear brothers and sisters,

Today's audience falls on the feast of St. Catherine of Siena, the patron saint of Italy together with St. Francis of Assisi. The memory of the humble and wise Dominican virgin fills the hearts of us all with spiritual exultation and makes us thrill with joy in the Holy Spirit, because the Lord of heaven and earth has revealed his secrets to the simple (cf. Lk. 10:21). Catherine's message, animated by pure faith, fervent love and tireless dedication to the Church, concerns each of us and sweeps us along sweetly to generous imitation. I am glad, therefore, to address a special greeting to the Italians present at this meeting and to the whole dear Italian people.

Listen, dear faithful, to these words of St. Catherine: "In the light of faith I acquire wisdom; in the light of faith I am strong, constant and persevering; in the light of faith I hope: I do not let myself stop along the road. This light teaches me the way" *(Dialogue,* chap. CLXVII).

Let us implore through her intercession an ever deeper and more ardent faith, so that

Christ may be the light of our way, of that of our families and of the whole of society, thus ensuring beloved Italy true peace, founded on justice and above all on respect for divine law, for which the great saint of Siena yearned.

1. We have already dedicated a series of reflections to the meaning of the words spoken by Christ in the Sermon on the Mount, in which He exhorts to purity of heart, calling attention even to the "lustful look." We cannot forget these words of Christ even when it is a question of the vast sphere of artistic culture, particularly that of a visual and spectacular character, as also when it is a question of the sphere of "mass" culture—so significant for our times —connected with the use of the audiovisual communications media. We said recently that the above-mentioned sphere of man's activity is sometimes accused of "pornovision," just as the accusation of "pornography" is made with regard to literature. Both facts take place by going beyond the limit of shame, that is, of personal sensitivity with regard to what is connected with the human body, with its nakedness, when in the artistic work by means of the media of audiovisual production the right to the privacy of the body in its masculinity or femininity is violated, and—in the last analysis—when that intimate and constant destination to the gift and to mutual donation, which is inscribed in that femininity and masculinity through the whole structure of the being-man, is violated. That deep inscription, or

rather incision, decides the nuptial meaning of the body, that is, the fundamental call it receives to form a "communion of persons" and to participate in it.

THE HUMAN BODY
AS MODEL OR SUBJECT

2. It is obvious that in works of art, or in the products of audiovisual artistic reproduction, the above-mentioned constant destination to the gift, that is, that deep inscription of the meaning of the human body, can be violated only in the intentional order of the reproduction and the representation; it is a question, in fact—as has already been previously said—of the human body as model or subject. However, if the sense of shame and personal sensitivity is offended in these cases, that happens because of their transfer to the dimension of "social communication," therefore, owing to the fact that what, in man's rightful feeling, belongs and must belong strictly to the interpersonal relationship—which is linked, as has already been pointed out, with the "communion of persons itself," and in its sphere corresponds to the interior truth of man, and so also to the complete truth about man—becomes, so to speak, public property.

At this point it is not possible to agree with the representatives of so-called naturalism, who demand the right to "everything that is human" in works of art and in the products of artistic reproduction, affirming that they act in this way in the name of the realistic truth about man. It is precisely this truth about man—the whole truth about man—that makes it necessary to take into consideration both the sense of the privacy of the body and the consistency of the gift connected with the masculinity and femininity of the body itself, in which the mystery of man, peculiar to the interior structure of the person, is reflected. This truth about man must be taken into consideration also in the artistic order, if we want to speak of a full realism.

VALUE OF BODY
IN INTERPERSONAL COMMUNION

3. In this case, therefore, it is evident that the deep governing rule related to the "communion of persons" is in profound agreement with the vast and differentiated area of "communication." The human body in its nakedness—as we stated in the preceding analyses (in which we referred to Genesis 2:25)—understood as a manifestation of the person and as his gift, that is, a sign of trust and donation to the other person, who is conscious of the gift, and who is chosen and resolved to respond to it in an equally personal way, becomes the source of a particular interpersonal "communication."

As has already been said, this is a particular communication in humanity itself. That interpersonal communication penetrates deeply into the system of communion *(communio per-sonarum)*, and at the same time grows from it and develops correctly within it. Precisely because of the great value of the body in this system of interpersonal "communion," to make of the body in its nakedness—which expresses precisely "the element" of the gift —the object-subject of the work of art or of the audiovisual reproduction, is a problem which is not only aesthetic, but at the same time also ethical. In fact, that "element of the gift" is, so to speak, suspended in the dimension of an unknown reception and an unforeseen response, and thereby it is in a way "threatened" in the order of intention, in the sense that it may become an anonymous object of "appropriation," an object of abuse. Precisely for this reason the integral truth about man constitutes in this case, the foundation of the norm according to which the good or evil of determined actions, of behavior, of morals and situations, is modeled. The truth about man, about what is particularly personal and interior in him—precisely because of his body and his sex (femininity-masculinity)—creates here precise limits which it is unlawful to exceed.

RECOGNIZING LIMITS

4. These limits must be recognized and observed by the artist who makes the human body the object, model or subject of the work of art or of the audiovisual reproduction. Neither

he nor others who are responsible in this field have the right to demand, propose or bring it about that other men, invited, exhorted or admitted to see, to contemplate the image, should violate those limits together with them, or because of them. It is a question of the image, in which that which in itself constitutes the content and the deeply personal value, that which belongs to the order of the gift and of the mutual donation of person to person, is, as a subject, uprooted from its own authentic substratum, to become, through "social communication," an object and what is more, in a way, an anonymous object.

5. The whole problem of "pornovision" and "pornography," as can be seen from what is said above, is not the effect of a puritanical mentality or of a narrow moralism, just as it is not the product of a thought imbued with Manichaeism. It is a question of an extremely important, fundamental sphere of values, before which man cannot remain indifferent because of the dignity of humanity, the personal character and the eloquence of the human body. All those contents and values, by means of works of art and the activity of the audiovisual media, can be modeled and studied, but also can be distorted and destroyed "in the heart" of man. As can be seen, we find ourselves continually within the orbit of the words spoken by Christ in the Sermon on the Mount. Also the problems which we are dealing with here must be examined in the light of

those words, which consider a look that springs from lust as "adultery committed in the heart."

It seems, therefore, that reflection on these problems, which are important to "create a climate favorable to education to chastity," constitutes an indispensable appendage to all the preceding analyses which we have dedicated to this subject in the course of the numerous Wednesday meetings.

Ethical Responsibilities in Art

General audience of May 6, 1981.

1. In the Sermon on the Mount Christ spoke the words to which we have devoted a series of reflections in the course of almost a year. Explaining to His listeners the specific meaning of the commandment: "You shall not commit adultery," Christ expressed Himself as follows: "But I say to you that everyone who looks at a woman lustfully has already committed adultery with her in his heart" (Mt. 5:28). The above-mentioned words seem to refer also to the vast spheres of human culture, especially those of artistic activity, with which we have already recently dealt in the course of some of the Wednesday meetings. Today it is opportune for us to dedicate the final part of these reflections to the problem of the relationship between the *ethos* of the image—or of the description—and the *ethos* of the viewing and listening, reading or other forms of cognitive reception with which one meets the content of the work of art or of audio-vision understood in the broad sense.

THE BODY IN ART

2. And here we return once more to the problem already previously mentioned: whether and to what extent can the human body, in the

whole visible truth of its masculinity and femininity, be a subject of works of art and thereby a subject of that specific social "communication" for which these works are intended? This question refers even more to modern "mass" culture, connected with the audiovisual media. Can the human body be such a model-subject, since we know that with this is connected that objectivity "without choice" which we first called anonymity, and which seems to bring with it a serious potential threat to the whole sphere of meanings, peculiar to the body of man and woman because of the personal character of the human subject and the character of "communion" of interpersonal relations?

One can add at this point that the expressions "pornography" and "pornovision"—despite their ancient etymology—appeared in language relatively late. The traditional Latin terminology used the word *obscaena*, indicating in this way everything that should not appear before the eyes of spectators, what should be surrounded with opportune discretion, what cannot be presented to human view without any choice.

BODY, A MODEL-SUBJECT

3. Asking the preceding question, we realize that, *de facto*, in the course of whole periods of human culture and artistic activity,

the human body has been and is such a model-subject of visual works of art, just as the whole sphere of love between man and woman, and, connected with it, also the "mutual donation" of masculinity and femininity in their corporeal expression, has been, is and will be a subject of literary narrative. Such narration found its place even in the Bible, especially in the text of the "Song of Songs," which it will be opportune to take up again on another occasion. In fact, it should be noted that in the history of literature or art, in the history of human culture, this subject seems particularly frequent and is particularly important. In fact, it concerns a problem which in itself is great and important. We showed this right from the beginning of our reflections, following the scriptural texts, which reveal to us the proper dimension of this problem: that is, the dignity of man in his masculine and feminine corporeity, and the nuptial meaning of femininity and masculinity, inscribed in the whole interior—and at the same time visible —structure of the human person.

SPECIAL ETHICAL RESPONSIBILITY

4. Our preceding reflections did not intend to question the right to this subject. They aim merely at proving that its treatment is connected with a special responsibility which is not only artistic, but also ethical in nature. The artist who undertakes that theme in any sphere of art or through audiovisual media,

must be aware of the full truth of the object, of the whole scale of values connected with it; he must not only take them into account *in abstracto*, but also live them correctly himself. This corresponds also to that principle of "purity of heart," which in determined cases, must be transferred from the existential sphere of attitudes and ways of behavior to the intentional sphere of creation or artistic reproduction.

It seems that the process of this creation aims not only at making the model concrete (and in a way at a new "materializing"), but, at the same time, at expressing in such concretizing what can be called the creative idea of the artist, in which his interior world of values, and so also his living the truth of his object, is precisely manifested. In this process there takes place a characteristic transfiguration of the model or of the material and, in particular, of what is man, the human body in the whole truth of its masculinity or femininity. (From this point of view, as we have already mentioned, there is a very important difference, for example, between the painting or sculpture and the photograph or film.) The viewer, invited by the artist to look at his work, communicates not only with the concretizing, and so, in a sense, with a new "materializing" of the model or of the material, but at the same time communicates with the truth of the object which the author, in his artistic "materializing," has succeeded in expressing with his own specific media.

ELEMENT OF SUBLIMATION
IN TRUE ART

5. In the course of the various eras, beginning from antiquity—and above all in the great period of Greek classical art—there are works of art whose subject is the human body in its nakedness, and the contemplation of which makes it possible to concentrate, in a way, on the whole truth of man, on the dignity and the beauty—also the "suprasensual" beauty—of his masculinity and femininity. These works bear within them, almost hidden, an element of sublimation, which leads the viewer, through the body, to the whole personal mystery of man. In contact with these works, where we do not feel drawn by their content to "looking lustfully," about which the Sermon on the Mount speaks, we learn in a way that nuptial meaning of the body which corresponds to, and is the measure of, "purity of heart." But there are also works of art, and perhaps even more often reproductions, which arouse objection in the sphere of man's personal sensitivity—not because of their object, since the human body in itself always has its inalienable dignity—but because of the quality or way of its reproduction, portrayal, artistic representation. The various coefficients of the work or the reproduction can be decisive with regard to that way and that quality, as well as multiple circumstances, often more of a technical nature than an artistic one.

It is well known that through all these elements the very fundamental intentionality of the work of art or of the product of the respective media becomes, in a way, accessible to the viewer, as to the listener or the reader. If our personal sensitivity reacts with objection and disapproval, it is because in that fundamental intentionality, together with the concretizing of man and his body, we discover as indispensable for the work of art or its reproduction, his simultaneous reduction to the level of an object, an object of "enjoyment," intended for the satisfaction of concupiscence itself. And that is contrary to the dignity of man also in the intentional order of art and reproduction. By analogy, the same thing must be applied to the various fields of artistic activity—according to the respective specific character—as also to the various audiovisual media.

CREATING AN ATMOSPHERE

6. Paul VI's Encyclical *Humanae vitae* (no. 22) emphasizes the "need to create an atmosphere favorable to education in chastity"; and with this he intends to affirm that the way of living the human body in the whole truth of its masculinity and femininity must correspond to the dignity of this body and to its significance in building the communion of persons. It can be said that this is one of the fundamental dimensions of human culture, understood as an affirmation which ennobles everything that is human. Therefore we have dedicated this brief

sketch to the problem which, in synthesis, could be called that of the *ethos* of the image. It is a question of the image which serves as an extraordinary "visualization" of man, and which must be understood more or less directly. The sculpted or painted image expresses man "visually"; the play or the ballet expresses him "visually" in another way, the film in another way; even literary work, in its own way, aims at arousing interior images, using the riches of the imagination or of human memory. So what we have called the "ethos of the image" cannot be considered apart from the correlative element, which we would have to call the "ethos of seeing." Between the two elements is contained the whole process of communication, independently of the vastness of the circles described by this communication, which, in this case, is always "social."

7. The creation of the atmosphere favorable to education in chastity contains these two elements; it concerns, so to speak, a reciprocal circuit which takes place between the image and the seeing, between the ethos of the image and the ethos of seeing. Just as the creation of the image, in the broad and differentiated sense of the term, imposes on the author, artist or reproducer, obligations not only of an aesthetic, but also of an ethical nature, so "looking," understood according to the same broad analogy, imposes obligations on the one who is the recipient of the work.

True and responsible artistic activity aims at overcoming the anonymity of the human body as an object "without choice," seeking (as has already been previously said), through creative effort, such an artistic expression of the truth about man in his feminine and masculine corporeity, which is, so to speak, assigned as a task to the viewer and, in the wider range, to every recipient of the work. It depends on him, in his turn, to decide whether to make his own effort to approach this truth, or to remain merely a superficial "consumer" of impressions, that is, one who exploits the meeting with the anonymous body-subject only at the level of sensuality which, by itself, reacts to its object precisely "without choice."

We conclude here this important chapter of our reflections on the theology of the body, whose starting point was the words spoken by Christ in the Sermon on the Mount: words valid for the man of all times, for the "historical" man, and valid for each one of us.

The reflections on the theology of the body would not be complete, however, if we did not consider other words of Christ, namely, those with which He refers to the future resurrection. So we propose to devote the next cycle of our considerations to them.

INDEX

Also by Pope John Paul II

Address of Pope John Paul II to the General Assembly of the United Nations
20 pages; 30¢ — EP0005

Apostolic Constitution on Ecclesiastical Universities and Faculties (Sapientia Christiana)
64 pages; 50¢ — EP0847

Apostolic Exhortation on Catechesis in Our Time (Catechesi Tradendae)
68 pages; 60¢ — EP0185

The Freedom of Conscience and Religion
12 pages; 25¢ — EP0489

Instruction Concerning Worship of the Eucharistic Mystery
16 pages; 25¢ — EP0605

Letter to All Bishops of the Church and to All Priests of the Church
34 pages; 25¢ — EP0688

On the Mercy of God (Dives in Misericordia)
52 pages; 50¢ — EP0863

On the Mystery and Worship of the Eucharist (Dominicae Cenae)
40 pages; 35¢ — EP0895

The Redeemer of Man (Redemptor Hominis)
64 pages; 50¢ — EP0978

Redemptor Hominis (Polish)
64 pages; 50¢ — EP0979

Collections of talks of His Holiness, Pope John Paul II, compiled and indexed by the Daughters of St. Paul unless otherwise indicated.

Africa—Apostolic Pilgrimage
cloth $8.00; paper $7.00 — EP0025

Brazil—Journey in the Light of the Eucharist
cloth $8.00; paper $7.00 — EP0175

The Far East Journey of Peace and Brotherhood
cloth $8.00; paper $7.00 — EP0485

France—Message of Peace, Trust, Love and Faith
cloth $5.00; paper $3.50 — EP0488

Germany, Pilgrimage of Unity and Peace
cloth $6.00; paper $5.00 — EP0515

I Believe in Youth, Christ Believes in Youth
cloth $4.95; paper $3.95 — EP0586

Ireland—In the Footsteps of St. Patrick
cloth $3.95; paper $2.95 — EP0675

Original Unity of Man and Woman
Catechesis on the Book of Genesis
Preface by Donald W. Wuerl
cloth $4.00; paper $3.00 — EP0896

Pilgrim to Poland
cloth $5.00; paper $3.50 — EP0955

Pope John Paul II—A Visit to Anchorage, Alaska
A pictorial album of the Pope's visit to Anchorage.
cloth $12.00 — EP0801

Pope John Paul II—He Came to Us As a Father
cloth $14.95 — EP0957

Puebla—A Pilgrimage of Faith
cloth $3.00; paper $2.00 — EP0976

Servant of Truth—Messages of John Paul II
cloth $9.95; paper $8.95 — RA0164

Talks of John Paul II
With foreword by His Eminence, John Cardinal Krol
cloth $7.95; paper $6.95 — RA0188

Turkey—Ecumenical Pilgrimage
cloth $3.50; paper $2.50 — EP1085

U.S.A.—The Message of Justice, Peace and Love
cloth $5.95; paper $4.95 — EP1095

Visible Signs of the Gospel
cloth $4.00; paper $2.95 — EP1098

The Whole Truth About Man
Edited and with an introduction by Rev. James V. Schall, S.J.
cloth $7.95; paper $6.95 — EP1099

"You Are My Favorites"
cloth $6.95 — EP1125

"You Are the Future, You Are My Hope"
cloth $4.95; paper $3.95 — EP1120

Set Apart for Service
cloth $4.00; paper $3.00 — EP0999

Give Your Life with Joy
cloth $2.25; paper $1.25 — EP0515

Through the Priestly Ministry, the Gift of Salvation, Vol. I
cloth $12.95; paper $11.95 — EP1055

Through the Priestly Ministry, the Gift of Salvation, Vol. II
cloth $12.95; paper $11.95 — EP1056

Africa—Land of Promise, Land of Hope
cloth $5.00; paper $3.50 — EP0027

Healing and Hope
cloth $5.00; paper $3.50 — EP0545

Faithfulness to the Gospel
cloth $4.50; paper $3.50 — EP0482

The Family: Center of Life and Love
Compiled and indexed by the Daughters of St. Paul
   The messages of Popes Paul VI, John Paul I and John Paul II regarding family life in the modern world reflect the particular role which the family is called to play in the entire plan of salvation.
cloth $6.00; paper $5.00 — EP0484

To the Church in America
   A collection of papal addresses by Popes John Paul II, John Paul I and Paul VI given to the Church in America. Published at the request of the Holy See. Indexed by the Daughters of St. Paul.
cloth $4.00; paper $3.00 — EP1065

Daughters of St. Paul

IN MASSACHUSETTS
50 St. Paul's Ave., Jamaica Plain, Boston, MA 02130;
617-522-8911; 617-522-0875.
172 Tremont Street, Boston, MA 02111; 617-426-5464;
617-426-4230.

IN NEW YORK
78 Fort Place, Staten Island, NY 10301; 212-447-5071; 212-447-5086.
59 East 43rd Street, New York, NY 10017; 212-986-7580.
625 East 187th Street, Bronx, NY 10458; 212-584-0440.
525 Main Street, Buffalo, NY 14203; 716-847-6044.

IN NEW JERSEY
Hudson Mall — Route 440 and Communipaw Ave.,
Jersey City, NJ 07304; 201-433-7740.

IN CONNECTICUT
202 Fairfield Ave., Bridgeport, CT 06604; 203-335-9913.

IN OHIO
2105 Ontario Street (at Prospect Ave.), Cleveland, OH 44115;
216-621-9427.
25 E. Eighth Street, Cincinnati, OH 45202; 513-721-4838;
513-421-5733.

IN PENNSYLVANIA
1719 Chestnut Street, Philadelphia, PA 19103; 215-568-2638.

IN VIRGINIA
1025 King Street, Alexandria, VA 22314; 703-683-1741;
703-549-3806.

IN FLORIDA
2700 Biscayne Blvd., Miami, FL 33137; 305-573-1618.

IN LOUISIANA
4403 Veterans Memorial Blvd., Metairie, LA 70002; 504-887-7631;
504-887-0113.
1800 South Acadian Thruway, P.O. Box 2028, Baton Rouge, LA 70821;
504-343-4057; 504-381-9485.

IN MISSOURI
1001 Pine Street (at North 10th), St. Louis, MO 63101; 314-621-0346;
314-231-1034.

IN ILLINOIS
172 North Michigan Ave., Chicago, IL 60601; 312-346-4228;
312-346-3240.

IN TEXAS
114 Main Plaza, San Antonio, TX 78205; 512-224-8101.

IN CALIFORNIA
1570 Fifth Ave., San Diego, CA 92101; 619-232-1442.
46 Geary Street, San Francisco, CA 94108; 415-781-5180.

IN HAWAII
1143 Bishop Street, Honolulu, HI 96813; 808-521-2731.

IN ALASKA
750 West 5th Ave., Anchorage, AK 99501; 907-272-8183.

IN CANADA
3022 Dufferin Street, Toronto 395, Ontario, Canada.

IN ENGLAND
128, Notting Hill Gate, London W11 3QG, England.
133 Corporation Street, Birmingham B4 6PH, England.
5A-7 Royal Exchange Square, Glasgow G1 3AH, England.
82 Bold Street, Liverpool L1 4HR, England.

IN AUSTRALIA
58 Abbotsford Rd., Homebush, N.S.W. 2140, Australia